Does This Collar Make
My Butt Look Big?

In less time than it takes to cough up a hairball, you too can be fit, feline, and fabulous!

Does This Collar Make My Butt Look Big?

A Diet Book for Cats

DENA HARRIS

ILLUSTRATIONS BY ANN BOYAJIAN

TEN SPEED PRESS
Berkeley

Contents

For All the Fat Kitties Out There

The scale doesn't lie . . . but we suspect
the vet tech we scratched earlier
is adding weight on with her thumb.

Acknowledgments

From the Cat

A diet book for cats? Brilliant. What's next? A motivational book for slugs? Let's not create problems where there are none, people. Big is beautiful. And so I'd like to thank everyone who had a paw in making me the cat I am today: my brothers from another mother, Ben & Jerry; my super-sweet Aunt Jemima; Mrs. Paul; the wild man from the hood, Cap'n Crunch; Little Debbie (s'up girl?); Howard Johnson; Slim Jim; Little Caesar (Vegas, baby!); Russell Stover; and my main "what happens in the back alley stays in the back alley" partner in crime, Jimmy Dean. You have all touched my heart. At least that's what my cardiologist tells me.

And don't go thinking I'm endorsing this book, because I'm not. Sorry you wasted your money. Maybe you should have spent it on a gym membership instead—you seem to have a bit of a muffin top going on there. *Mmm . . . muffins.* Good-bye.

From the Human

Feline obesity is no joke. Unless I can profit from it in some way. Then it's extraordinarily funny.

I owe a world of thanks to many people. To my writing buddies—Christopher Laney, Steve Cushman, Edmund Schubert, Daniel Shirley, Rudy Daugherty, and the Madison Writers Group—thanks for always being there and helping me brainstorm twenty different ways to say "regurgitate." Props to Ron Culberson for early edits and puns. Love to best friend Trisha for feeding every stray cat that comes to her door. Shout out to the Sole Sisters for keeping me running when I insisted that eating a pound of dark chocolate dipped in almond butter was "research" for my latest cat diet book. And hugs to my mom, dad, and sister for making everyone they know buy my books.

To Winifred Golden at Castiglia Literary Agency and Lisa Westmoreland at Ten Speed Press—authors like to moan about how the good old days of being supported and nurtured by agents and editors are long gone. I can't relate—I've got a great team on my side.

I'm grateful to own (or be owned by) two fat cats, because without them, this book might not have happened.

And finally, there are no words to express my love and gratitude to my husband, Blair Harris. Thanks for letting me live the dream. Also, the cats' dishes are empty again. Fill them up, would you babe?

Cheers,

Dena

Introduction

Does This Collar Make My Butt Look Big? is *the* book for any cat hoping to transform into a lean, mean, sleeping machine. While other diet and exercise books encourage a healthy lifestyle based on portion control and exercise, this book promotes the more feline-friendly approach of "returning your calories to the earth" (also known as "blowing chunks").

This book is also a wake-up call for cats who just need to be, you know . . . awake. (Seriously, some of what we're saying here is important. Get up.)

Want to be as strong as a professional mouser? Ready to admit that hot and sexy belly that's been dragging on the floor the last few years maybe isn't so hot and sexy? On the following pages you'll find a stash of easy-to-use *purr*actical tips such as:

- **Eat whatever you want.** Just do what cats have done for centuries and disgorge a small mound of bones, fur, and grass someplace your humans will be sure to step in it.

- **Work in light cardio.** Twice daily, increase your heart rate by running in frenzied circles around the house as if you're being chased by a cat burglar or a veterinarian with a thermometer.

- **Seek out fresh, local food.** Protein still in its final death throes is always healthiest . . . like that vole in the backyard.

If you're ready for these secrets and more, keep reading. In less time than it takes to groom your backside, you too can be fit, feline, and fabulous!

Taking Stock: Where Are You Now?

Let's be honest. If you're reading this book, chances are you're sporting a little "junk in the kitty trunk." But are you actually "overweight"? Find out by rating your body using these definitions:

- **Plump.** The ground shakes when you approach. Not because people fear you, but just because . . . you're approaching.

- **Stocky.** It takes two or three leaps and a complicated system of grappling hooks for you to summit the bed.

- **Obese.** If we could tie a string to you and make you float, you'd fit right into the Macy's Thanksgiving Day parade.

- **Big boned.** Dinosaurs were big boned. Sasquatch is big boned. Pull up your kitty Piddle Pants[1] and face the truth: you're *fat*.

---

1. *Real item!*

Before Before There Was Diet Kibble . . .
A History of Fat Cats

It should come as no surprise that our feline ancestors, such as the European wild cat and African wild cat, didn't struggle with their weight. With no easy access to Trader Joe's Turkey & Giblets in Gravy—the nearest outlet was miles away—these cats were forced onto the plains and into caves to hunt and forage for food. Research reveals that the European cave lion, in an early adaptation of today's popular Paleo diet (see page 54), occasionally noshed on bear cubs. (This was before the petit fours rage swept the plains, ushering in an era of catnip-tart and mini-vole desserts.)

These days, pampered cats are more likely to snort a bowl of Friskies Party Mix than to take down a grizzly. (Although . . . snorting Friskies has made more then one cat hallucinate they *were* taking down a grizzly, only to wake up the next morning in a compromising position with the dog's Kong Teddy Bear toy. About that, perhaps the less said, the better.) In fact, more than 50 percent of felines are overweight—which of course means that 50 percent of felines are normal or underweight. How you see it depends on whether you're a "the bowl is half empty" or "the bowl is half full" kind of cat. Since you're reading a diet book, you're probably a "the bowl is *always* empty" kind of cat—which reminds us: FEED ME.

How does this affect you? You've got your blankie, your sunbeam, and unlimited access to the naughty cable channels while your humans are at work. Why should you care about being overweight? Because issues linked to obesity include diabetes, stroke, heart attack, and the mortification that comes with having to be weighed on the livestock scale behind the veterinarian's office.

> Confront those who don't want you to change. And by "confront," we mean show them your butt.

So where to begin? The first step (calm down—you don't actually have to stand up and go anywhere) is to test your knowledge. Take the quiz starting on page 6 to help you determine how much you know about shedding (*no, not that kind of shedding—if only it were that easy*) those unwanted pounds. Then grab a meal replacement bar,[2] turn the page, and let your weight-loss odyssey begin.

---

2. *Also known as "the fridge."*

Climbing the Feline Food Pyramid

Note: You may have unlimited quantities of anything that the dog appears interested in eating.

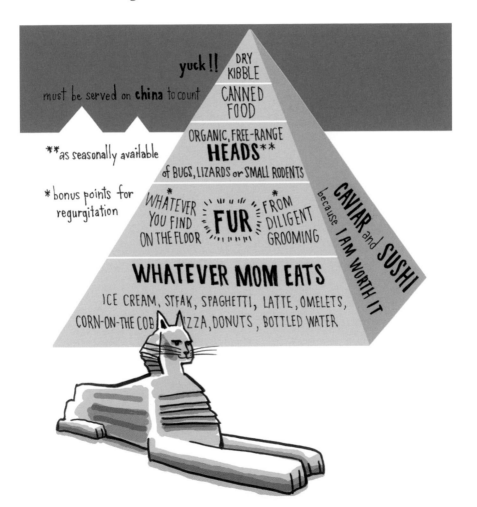

Quizzzz

Not all diets are created equal. This quiz will help determine what kind of dieter you are—or would be, if you ever actually committed to eating a little less—and which diet is best suited for your *purr*sonality type.

Instructions: Paw tap on the answer to each question that best describes your relationship to food and exercise.

1. How motivated are you to lose weight?
   a. *Zzzz*—Huh? Wha . . . ? Is it time to eat?
   b. Depends. Is there any sort of moist food reward if I lose the weight?
   c. What does this word "motivated" mean?
   d. Highly motivated (for about forty minutes every morning at 5:00 a.m.; then the buzz wears off)

2. Which is healthier—dark or white meat?
   a. Dark
   b. White
   c. I drown everything in gravy, so it doesn't really matter.

3. Do you eat for emotional reasons?
   a. Since I don't care about anything, I doubt it.
   b. My therapist doesn't think so.
   c. Maybe. Probably not. No, those aren't tears. I'm allergic to questions.
   d. Ha. *No.* I'm fine. Perfectly fine. Thanks for asking though, but I'm fine. Fine.

4. When I eat, I most resemble a

a. DustBuster (compact, goes everywhere, picks up every last bit)

b. Dyson Vacuum Cleaner (innovative technology!)

c. Shop-Vac (works on wet or dry food—industrial strength!)

d. Pimped-up Hoover (powerful suction!)

> Use motivational notes and reminders. Hang a "Hot Kitty" calendar nearby to remind you what you want to look like.

5. Is it better to cut calories or to exercise more?

a. Cut calories.

b. Exercise more.

c. What sort of sick *Sophie's Choice* game are you playing at?

6. Do you feel your eating is out of control?

a. Yes

b. No

c. *Mmrrgh-urgh-chew-chew.* (Swallow.) Sorry, what?

7. What is the best reason to be a vegetarian?

a. Poor hunting skills

b. Moral superiority

c. I hope to someday pen my own celebrity cookbook.

d. I oppose killing animals for food. Ha ha—kidding! Want to go halvsies on this baby mouse I caught?

8. When faint with hunger, what will most quickly revive you?
a. *TOO*-NAH. Now, please.
b. Canine rump roast
c. Quick hit of catnip
d. The sound of a can opener

9. What do you use to sauté your food?
a. A stick of butter
b. Cold-pressed, extra-virgin, sardine-flavored olive oil from the Tuscan region of Italy
c. Lard—and keep the fat jokes to yourself.
d. Saliva—drizzled generously over the pan

10. Cutting back on your morning coffee fix will help you lose weight:
a. True
b. False
c. Yeah, right—and then what would I have with my cigarette?
d. Maybe, but I'd lose my catlike reflexes.

11. Brushing my teeth after a meal . . .
a. Helps prevent snacking
b. Requires a straitjacket for physical restraint
c. Is best followed by a rinse of *His*sterine mouthwash[3]
d. Is a good way for someone to end up at the hospital getting treated for a cat bite

---

3. *"Kills the germs that cause rodent breath!"*

12. Eating kibble reduces stress.

    a. True

    b. False

    c. Only until the bowl starts to get empty. Then panic sets in.

13. A typical breakfast for me:

    a. Can it still be called "breakfast" if I don't wake up to eat it until 5 p.m.?

    b. There's kibble in my bowl. *What a surprise.*

    c. I like to carbo-load with a big bowl of Mice Krispies. Plus I like the squeaky sound they make when I add milk.

    d. Two goldfish, sunny side up

14. Reasons to avoid exercise:

    a. The treadmill is trying to kill me.

    b. The stability ball is trying to kill me.

    c. The Bowflex is trying to kill me.

    d. The kettle ball is trying to kill me.

    e. The exercise bands . . . not yet sure of their intent. But pretty sure they're trying to kill me.

15. Which best describes your eating habits?

    a. One big meal a day

    b. Two moderate meals a day

    c. Hourly grazing

    d. It's not a "habit," it's a competition, and I'm winning.

> *Diet Tip:*
> Hold off on urinating for as long as possible, then make a mad dash for the litter box. Feel the burn.

16. Do you eat out or prepare your own food?
   a. Eat out—humans force me to drag myself all the way into the kitchen.
   b. Prepare my own. I make a wicked sushi.[4]
   c. Since I insist on pushing my kibble out of my dish and onto the floor before I dine, I suppose "eat out."
   d. I like to bag some squirrels from the backyard for an easy takeout meal.

17. My body type is
   a. Pear shaped
   b. Apple shaped
   c. Square
   d. Hexagonal (the fat makes the fur stick out in odd ways)

18. Which of the following causes you the most anxiety?
   a. Doorbells
   b. Exam tables
   c. Empty food dish
   d. Feline baldness and wondering if you can pull off a comb-over

19. What is your weight loss goal?
   a. To trade a cow for some magic beans that produce a bean stalk that leads me to a castle where rolls of fat are considered sexy
   b. To lose enough weight to scale the parakeet cage without its tipping over

---

4. And no, I have no idea why the fish tank is empty. No thoughts whatsoever. None.

c. To make the dancing cockatoo stop singing, *"Fatty, fatty, two by four, can't fit through the cat flap door"* every time I try to go outside

d. To lose weight. (Seriously, this is basic stuff here. Are you even qualified to be asking these questions?)

20. My motivation for losing weight is

a. I want to rock out a belly ring

b. Swimsuit season is upon us

c. REVENGE

d. To be healthy. Just kidding. It's the belly ring, bikini, and REVENGE.

Results

MOSTLY A'S: THE COMATOSE CAT

Diet, schmiet. You don't know and, what's more, don't care about exercise or healthy eating. You enjoy living large and have no problem being called "Fatty," so long as the food dish stays full. And for the record, anyone who approaches you with diet kibble is going to lose an eye.

------------------------ RECOMMENDED DIETS ------------------------
YOU: On a Diet
The South Beach Diet

MOSTLY B'S: THE OCD CAT

Counting calories? Lining up your allotted kibbles for the day *just so* before swatting them down the hall? Tracking your daily stinkies deposit? You thrive on consistency. Rules, guidelines, and never ever, *ever* rearranging the furniture[5] are the principles on which you base your life. Unfortunately, you're full of excuses when it comes to sticking to a diet. Just remember, excuses won't buy you a smaller waistline. (Sucking in the belly when the tape measure goes around it, however, will.)

-------------------------- RECOMMENDED DIETS --------------------------
Eat Right for Your Blood Type
French Women Don't Get Fat . . . But Their Cats Do

MOSTLY C'S: THE ADD CAT

Your weight is up; it's down. It's up; it's down. What's an ADD kitty to do? You're motivated to lose the weight, until hunger kicks in. Then it's like a scene out of *The Hunger Games* where booby traps are laid in an all-out survival effort to be the first and last cat standing at the food dish.

-------------------------- RECOMMENDED DIETS --------------------------
Paleo Diet
The Zone
Raw Food Diet and the Living Food Movement

---

5. *Why? Why would someone do that?*

MOSTLY D'S: THE CHRONIC DIETER

Your love handles may runneth over, but you haven't given up. Hope springs eternal as you pounce on every new fad (and food crumb) to cross your path, convinced *this* will be the diet that proportions your body so you no longer look like a witch doctor shrank your head.

------------------------ RECOMMENDED DIETS ------------------------
Master Your Meta*purrr*lism
Catty Craig/Weight Stalkers

COMBINATION: PSYCHO KITTY

The daily deluge of diet options makes the space between your ears hurt. You, more than any other feline, would benefit from no-nonsense guidelines. Meanwhile, a diet plan involving yarn or fishing wire to keep you tied up and away from the food dish would be helpful.

------------------------ RECOMMENDED DIETS ------------------------
The Mayo Clinic Diet
Cleanses
Hannibal Lecter fiberglass restraint mask

NO ANSWERS/REFUSAL TO PARTICIPATE IN THE QUIZ: FAT CAT FOR LIFE

We won't even bother trying to convince you of the health benefits of losing a few pounds. Go back to sleep. We'll wake you when it's time for dinner.

THE
Comatose Cat

Are you fat? Yes. Feeling a little hostile about dieting? Yes.
(Ow. Hey, no scratching.) Motivated to change your ways?
Not so much.

For all the good they may do, here are the recommended
diet plans for you.

YOU: On a Diet

The South Beach Diet

YOU: On a Diet: A Cat's Manual for ~~Waist~~ Waste Management

Let's get real:

- Do you find yourself gasping for air when attempting something aerobic, like standing?

- Are you guilty of midnight "sleepwalking" raids on the cans of curried lamb and rice?[1]

- Is your energy level so low your humans have dug a hole in the back yard more than once, thinking you were dead?

If you answered "yes" to any of these questions, congratulations on being awake. But also, keep reading. You are a comatose kitty, and this diet is for you.

---

1. *Suuuure you were asleep. We believe you. (Wink-wink.)*

For the first time, scientists are unraveling diet secrets (the secrets were wrapped up in a big ball of yarn—who knew?) about why certain felines struggle with their weight. The average house cat is 6 pounds overweight and more closely resembles a rotund garden gnome (yes, the very same one you've been stalking, over by the petunias) than the sleek, fleet-footed predator of the past. The aim of YOU: On a Diet is nothing less than to change the very behaviors that are making you fa—uh, extra furry.

You may be wondering whether going on a diet is truly necessary. The answer is yes. There's no pill that will make you thin, and even if there were, we'd have to force it down your throat only to have you cough it out at our feet moments later. Are you ready to shave inches off your waist (without having your fur shaved)? Then let's begin!

> Too little sleep can make you fat. Aim for at least twenty-two hours a day.

Part I: How It Works

The secret to YOU: On a Diet is the two-week reboot program. Relax. We understand your concerns about boots. They can be scary. However, though we much prefer Birkenstock sandals (good funky smell, and we know you derive great pleasure from cramming your face through the straps), "two-week Birkenstock program" doesn't have the same ring and, frankly, was attracting too many hippies.

During this two-week reboot you will change your eating patterns. You will eat whole foods (including heads, intestines, and tails) and break the cycle of craving unhealthy foods such as pizza, dairy, and whatever the dog eats. You'll eat every twenty minutes, assuming you're awake and can figure out how to work the latch on the cupboard where the kitty chow is kept.

STAGE I: TWO-WEEK REBOOT INSTRUCTIONS

Step 1: Measure your waistline. Get a soft measuring tape and roll it out flat on the floor. Next—LOOK OUT! THERE'S A SNAKE! POUNCE ON IT! Wait, false alarm. That's just the measuring tape—NO! IT'S A SNAKE! SNAKE! ATTACK!! Oops, our bad. It's just that our feline instinct is to—IT MOVED! KILL IT! KILL IT! KILL IT!

Um, you know what? Forget the tape. Just take your best guess at what your waist measurement is and write that down.

Step 2: Walk thirty minutes a day. Does it have to be thirty minutes all at once? No. Does kneading your paws one by one into the soft flesh of your person's belly count as "walking"? Yes. Does rappelling up the fridge to get to the Key lime pie in the freezer count as well? Sure, why not?

Step 3: Automate two meals per day. Diets fail due to too much variety. Keep it simple and eat the same meals over and over. Oh, wait— what's that you say? Just that you and every cat on the planet already do this? Because *heaven forbid your person take time away from watching* The Bachelorette *to fix a meal that involves more than dipping a never-washed plastic cup into an open fifteen-pound bag of stale kibble, dumping* *it into a never-washed bowl, and congratulating herself on being the Betty Crocker of the feline world.* Whew! Sorry. That one's been festering for a while.

Step 4: Take your "before" pics. You'll want to take some "before " pictures of your zaftig feline form. That way you'll have something handy to shred in anger and disgust if and—

> Try grilling, sautéing, or baking your food, but be sure to ask permission to use the stove first.

let's be honest—*when* this diet doesn't work. Also, in ten years you'll look back at this photo and *wish* you still had that body.

Once the reboot is complete, you'll have your carbohydrate, sugar, and carpet fiber cravings under control. Now we move into Stage II—Waste Management.

STAGE II: WASTE MANAGEMENT

There are two ways to lose weight. You can eat less and exercise more—which, being a comatose kitty, we know isn't going to work for you—or you can eat as much as you want and figure out new and inventive ways to expel it. Guess which option we chose?

Note: You'll want to stock up on extra litter before undertaking this portion of the program, and buying a few scented candles wouldn't hurt.

Ready to move things along? Here's a list of natural foods for you to try:

- Parsley • Dandelions • Melons • Asparagus • Kitty grass
- Anything the dog eats. He seems to poop a lot.

Once you've gulped down your laxative of choice, relax, but don't stray too far from the litter box. Think of it as a calorie burner—you're going to get your paws dirty with all the burying you'll need to do. On the bright side, you'll have fun chasing people out of the room with your kitty poots of death.

Conclusion

As we leave you—Hey! You can at least stay awake until we say goodbye—here are some final YOU: On a Diet strategies to incorporate into daily life.

- Eat constantly throughout the day, even if you have to wake up to do it.

- Drink water before each meal. If you don't like water, don't worry. Splashing around in the water dish and making a mess counts as well.

- Keep emergency snacks on hand, like mice, toast crumbs, and the scrambled egg you snagged in the snatch-and-grab raid on yesterday's breakfast.

- Track how hungry you are on a scale of 1 to 10. Any time you go above a 1, eat immediately, before fatigue and hallucinations set in.

- Don't beat up on yourself if you make a mistake. That's what the dog is there for.

- Use a smaller food bowl so it appears your meals are bigger. Or buy larger kibble.

- Find a diet buddy. Give him a paw smack whenever you stray from your diet, as he's obviously not doing his job.

- Strength train one muscle group a day. Raise a paw; lower a paw. Raise a tail; lower a tail. Suck in your gut . . . ooh, that one hurts. Never mind.

- Stretch daily to prevent injury. The best time to do this is when waking up from a catnap before rolling over to go to sleep for the night.

And remember, whether you succeed or fail on this particular plan, we suggest you go ahead and tell everyone you've lost weight. Others will be impressed, thinking you have willpower they don't, and—in a fit of carb-craving jealousy—will go order a ten-taco special and gain twelve pounds, making you appear more svelte, regardless.

The South Beach Diet

Hmmm. You're still reading? That must mean the YOU: On a Diet plan didn't work for you. (Or else you're still waiting for the asparagus and kitty grass to kick in.) No worries. The South Beach Diet has a lot to offer cats who find it difficult to stay awake long enough to digest the bad fats fed to them by their owners[2] (and fed to them by the old lady up the street who takes pity on them because she thinks they're strays). Besides, any diet with a title resembling a warm litter box gets a paws up from us.

This chapter will cover the three phases of the famed South Beach Diet, as well as diet success stories to motivate you. However, before

---

2. *When presented with bad fats, try scolding them. "No! That's a bad, bad fat! Time out for you."*

beginning this—or really, any diet—you must *identify your goals.* WHY do you want to lose weight? (And don't give us that "Because it's bikini season" line. We all know you react to water like a fast-food junkie does to tofu.)

It's time to dig deep and explore your feelings. *Feelings.* Those swells of emotion that—what? No, we're not saying feelings will literally make you swell. Good grief. Feelings are simply mental sensations that— excuse me? Don't walk away from me when I'm trying to explain to you what feelings are. Hey! Do NOT show me your butt. Put your tail down right now! That's just gross. You are a *bad kitty.* You hear me? Bad kitty!

Fine, we won't talk about feelings. (I'm just saying that all this repression is probably what's making you fat.) But you do need to identify the reasons behind why you want to lose weight. For example, maybe you're hoping to . . .

- Stop getting stuck in the pet door?
- Fit into the old collars you've been hanging on to for years?
- Wear the "sexy human" Halloween costume you bought last year but were too embarrassed to be seen in?
- Have that neighbor kid quit referring to you as "Jabba"?

The South Beach Diet can make all of these your reality. Simply adhere[3] to the diet guidelines outlined in the pages that follow.

---

3. *Use sticky paws tape if needed.*

What Is the South Beach Diet?

Heart-healthy, low-glycemic (you would not *believe* how much sugar is in catnip), and low-fat, the South Beach Diet allows you to meander back and forth between phases—perfect for comatose kitties who sleep so long they can't remember what phase they were in the last time they were awake.

Fair warning: Just because the word "beach" is in there does not mean this is some posh litter box retreat. You will work and suffer and *starve* on this diet, which is good—that's how you know it's working.

The diet starts out with a lot of restrictions, but the rules are simple: Don't eat anything that tastes good.[4] Just follow the three phases outlined below.

Phase 1

This phase involves the complete denial of all foods that make you purr. The only sustenance allowed is kibble that tastes like corrugated cardboard, and then in portions that are only large enough to satisfy a gerbil. You'll likely experience increased hallway pacing and an unsettling desire to join the dog in lowering yourself to beg for food.

Separate your short-term and long-term goals. Short-term goals are things like "Stay awake long enough to stay on the diet"; a long-term goal might be . . . zzzzz. . . . Huh? What? Sorry, dozed off there for a minute. You were saying . . . ?

4. *However, if you eat something that tastes like processed cardboard and induces an immediate gag reflex, you're permitted unlimited quantities. Enjoy.*

Phase 2

Here we add back in some of the foods you love. But—and this is important—not enough food to ever really make you feel full. Some destruction of furniture and personal property, such as shredding your humans' shoes (while their feet are still in them), is to be expected.

Phase 3

This phase includes plenty of "me time" in solitary confinement (that is, the guest bathroom), where you'll be placed after you go on a catnip-induced dust-bunny killing spree, having been denied everything but diet kibble for three months.

Of course, the test of any diet is, does it work? Knowing the doubting tomcat that you are, we've pulled together some unpaid[5] testimonials from cats who have successfully followed the South Beach Diet.

Success Stories

MY SOUTH BEACH DIET SUCCESS STORY: PRINCESS WHISKERS

Starting Weight: 22 pounds

Ending Weight: 13 pounds

Biggest Challenge: Controlling between-meal snacking

My Story: I had just been taken in off the streets and was having

---

5. *At least not in cash. Some ear scratching may have been involved.*

trouble adjusting to indoor life. Having food available 24/7 was a new experience for me, and I found myself packing on the pounds. I went from an eight-pound feral to a twenty-two-pound pussycat in a matter of months! I started avoiding mirrors—and not just because there was always a fat, hissing cat there staring back at me. I'm living proof that if you stick with this diet, you *will* lose the weight. I was a yowling, miserable mess on this diet, but since that wasn't terribly different from my everyday persona, no one really noticed.

Diet Tip: Take a mouthful of kibble and let it slowly dissolve. People will become convinced you're holding something in your mouth that's either poisonous or half alive, and they'll chase you around the house, thus forcing you to get in some cardio.

> Keep portable, healthy snacks on hand, such as gerbils in those clear plastic balls.

MY SOUTH BEACH DIET SUCCESS STORY: MR. NIBS

Starting Weight: 18 pounds

Ending Weight: 12 pounds

Biggest Challenge: Resisting the urge to maim the humans who put me on this God-forsaken eating plan

My Story: I have a weakness for moist food. You know how some cats can take a bite or two and walk away? Not me. Even thinking about a seafood medley gets my taste buds salivating. That's why I never thought this diet would work for me. The only thing that made it possible was the fact that I couldn't work the can opener.

I'm thin now, though. And when other cats ask me, "Was losing the weight worth it?" I tell them, "Hell, no!" I want my moist food back. I hate the people who did this to me, and I spend my days plotting my revenge. They'll learn the hard way what happens when you come between Mr. Nibs and his Seafood Variety Pack. They will pay; oh, how they will pay!

Diet Tip: If you have a chance to bolt through an open door and take your chances living on the street versus suffering through this diet, do it.

MY SOUTH BEACH DIET SUCCESS STORY: GINGER

Starting Weight: 19 pounds

Ending Weight: 22 pounds

Biggest Challenge: Convincing people I'm not fat, just big boned

My Story: I lost six pounds on the South Beach Diet . . . and gained back eight. What did I do wrong? Nothing! I'm never to blame! I'm *purr*fection *purr*sonified. If the stupid diet doesn't work, it's not my fault. You're upsetting me with all this talk of me being fat. Let's go get some gelato and just pretend this never happened.

Diet Tip: I *told you*, I don't need to diet! I'm not fat! I'm just big boned!

For the Comatose Cat: Exercises You Can (Almost) Do in Your Sleep

It's time to wake up and smell the sweat. You may think you don't like to work out, but what if rolling over to follow the sunbeam counts as a workout? How about racing down the stairs every time you hear the whirr of the can opener? Surely the full-body muscle clench you engage in every time you see a squirrel or the stupid cat from next door in your yard is burning up the calories?

No, none of that counts? Then forget it. You're not exercising.

> Jump-start your exercise plan! Jump up, then go back to sleep. Repeat every twelve hours as necessary.

THE
OCD Cat

Just as you wouldn't enter a room without first scoping it out for Stranger Danger—or for Aunt Dorothy, who smells like wet dog—you're not going to partake in just any diet plan. You need specifics: What's involved? Are there any long-term effects? Has it been laboratory tested (on dogs)? And are the people preparing your food thoroughly washing their hands and not just saying that they did?

Lighten up, kitty. Here are the recommended diet plans for you and your obsessive ways.

Eat Right for Your Blood Type

French Women Don't Get Fat . . . But Their Cats Do

Eat Right For Your Blood Type

Oh, snap. Did someone say blood? Cheers! We love a good red.

This diet is right up an anal-retentive cat's alley, allowing you to match the food you eat to your blood type. The obvious downside is that for this diet to work, someone, at some point, is going to have to take blood from you.[1] The benefit, of course, is that once you know your blood type, you can eat accordingly, and the weight will drop off like a Pomeranian tossed off a bridge.

A Quick Survey of Blood Types

- **Blood Type O.** This blood type is the universal donor. Not surprisingly, this universality extends to your food. You should eat anything and everything you can get your paws on, including dental

---

1. *We don't, however, suggest you give in without a fight. Martial arts combat training has proven highly useful to cats in veterinary settings, with the added bonus that leaping off exam tables and scurrying around the legs of vet techs burns off additional calories.*

floss, which can be regurgitated at a later time, preferably right before dinner guests arrive.

- **Blood Type A.** This blood type thrives on a primarily vegetarian diet. Yeah. If this is you, you're screwed.

- **Blood Type B.** This blood type thrives on a mixed diet of meat, fish, and dairy. *Jackpot!*

- **Blood Type AB.** It doesn't matter what you thrive on, because your reaction to everything is a knee-jerk *"Blech! Ick! No, I won't eat it!"*

The Type O Profile

Type O cats are natural-born hunters. Although powerful, your type can become easily stressed and startled when your diet gets off kilter.

TYPE O PERSONALITY

Very practical and decisive. If you want to be fed, you want to be fed NOW. You're also very intuitive, sensing when someone you love is upset or knowing when it's precisely an hour before you're due at the vet so you can go into hiding.

> Don't rely on the dog to be your diet buddy. How much motivation can you get from someone who eats out of your litter box?

TYPE O DIET

Eat everything in sight.

MANAGE YOUR TYPE O STRESS

Your Type O ancestry lends itself to the classic "fight or flight" response. The "flight" response can lead to destructive behaviors involving doorframes and sofa cushions, and we won't even go into what you did with the toilet paper.

The best way for a Type O to manage stress is to stay active. Toys involving movement, laser lights, or jingly sounds will keep your mind occupied and your body relaxed.

> Fool yourself into fullness. Eat a lot of rubber bands. No calories, and the bands will expand in your stomach, knotting around your gut and making you feel full. Or constipated.

LIVE RIGHT!

In addition to eating foods that are right for your type, here are a few key lifestyle strategies for Type O kitties:

- To avoid putting claw marks on the ceiling every time the doorbell rings, eat small meals frequently.

- Eat all meals seated at your food dish. Lying down counts too.

- Occasionally raise your head out of the food bowl between bites to *breathe*.

- Feeling anxious? Do something physical. Just make sure it doesn't involve toilet paper.

The Type A Profile

If Type O's are the hunters, Type A's are the gatherers. Think sturdy pioneer barn cat. Sadly, type A's don't fare well with a meat diet. More broccoli?

THE TYPE A PERSONALITY

Forget excitement. You thrive best in an orderly, structured, no-surprises environment. You'd do well as a cat in a nursing home, provided there aren't too many close encounters with a rocking chair.

TYPE A DIET

You may find it challenging to give up meat. We have no suggestions for you. Maybe try yoga or some deep-breathing exercises to take your mind off the fact that it sucks to be you.

MANAGE YOUR TYPE A STRESS

Unfortunately, you were born into the world a bit of a basket case. Stress is as natural to you as breathing. This can lead to obsessive-compulsive behaviors such as excessive grooming to the point of licking yourself bald.[2] To control your natural "I'm freaking out!" response to life, limit your exposure to the following:

- People
- Loud noise
- Celebrity gossip

---

2. Unless you're a Sphynx cat—not a good look.

- *Shark Week* TV programming
- Extreme weather conditions, such as alternatively lying on the air conditioning vent and in your sunbeam

LIVE RIGHT!

In addition to working a strand of worry beads incessantly and eating foods that are right for your type, here are a few key lifestyle strategies for Type A kitties:

- Cultivate creativity. Try your paw at art projects, perhaps decoupage from the toilet paper shreds left over from your Type O roommate's rampage.
- Establish a consistent schedule: eat, sleep, poop. Repeat.
- Don't lie awake in bed. When your eyes open, roll over and go back to sleep as soon as possible!
- Don't eat when you are anxious. If this means you have to wait to eat . . . well, that will just cause greater anxiety, so go ahead and eat.

The Type B Profile

All that matters is you get to eat meat, and the snooty Persian next door who's a Type A doesn't. Be sure to position the outdoor grill so the odor of grilled beef wafts in her direction.

THE TYPE B PERSONALITY

Adaptable best describes you, with an eager willingness to tolerate toddlers, teenagers, and even a pit bull with equanimity.

TYPE B DIET

You have the easiest time of all blood types when it comes to controlling your weight. You're able to eat a wide and varied diet, including goat, lamb, rabbit, and—if you can bring one down—venison. The only meat to avoid is chicken. Why? Because God can't give all the good fortune to just one blood type.

MANAGE YOUR TYPE B STRESS

One caution: If your diet gets out of whack (we *told* you eating chicken would have that effect on you!), you have a tendency toward depression. A "Goodbye cruel cat world; now watch as I fling myself off this mantel because I haven't been combed yet today" type of depression.[3]

LIVE RIGHT!

Don't be so laid-back that you don't participate in life. Here are a few key lifestyle strategies for Type B kitties:

- Experiment with martial arts. Ninja throwing stars make everything better.

- Find healthy ways to express your non-conformist side. Sit under a running shower. Help a baby bird back into its nest. Get an "I ♥ Dobermans" tattoo on your bicep.

> Set short-term goals, such as "run a lap around the couch by next Thursday."

---

3. Seriously, lay off the chicken.

- Ignore any suggestions from Type O kitties about the healing properties of toilet paper.

- Type B's are natural-born networkers. Engage in a community, neighborhood, or group activity that gives you a sense of connection, such as a scavenger hunt or group bathing.

- Be spontaneous. But not around Type A's. It freaks them out.

- As you age, you may suffer memory loss. Stay sharp by doing tasks that require concentration, such as carefully unraveling a thread on the new couch.

The Type AB Profile

You are a chameleon. No, you're still a cat. We just mean your blood is chameleon-like in that—look, don't get offended. It's a compliment. C'mon out from under the couch.

Getting extra sleep improves athletic performance. For Olympian-caliber athleticism, try to avoid being awake. Ever.

TYPE AB PERSONALITY

You are a combination of the A and B blood types. This makes you adaptable, yet you prefer routine. You also share Type O's love of adventure. Combine all these traits, and more often than not what we find is that *you* are the cat for whom the fire department must be called when you get stuck in a tree.

TYPE AB DIET

You do best with little meat and lots of fish: mahi-mahi, red snapper, salmon, sardines, and tuna. Sadly, most humans consider Mrs. Paul's fish sticks the height of culinary seafood dining.[4]

MANAGE YOUR TYPE AB STRESS

Exercise plays a critical component in managing your stress. Aim for three days a week of yoga. Many simple yoga poses can be done in bed, including *shavasana* (corpse pose), *balasana* (child's pose), *bhujangasana* (cobra pose), *adho mukha svanasana* (downward facing dog pose), and *hogho blankie shavasana* (all these covers are *mine* pose).

LIVE RIGHT!

In addition to blending into the furniture while you nap, here are a few key lifestyle strategies for Type AB kitties:

- Avoid highly competitive situations, such as double-dog-daring the neighbor's cat to see who can arch his back the highest.

- Never rush, even to the litter box. If you don't make it, cleanup is not your problem.

- Carve out "me" time. This can be time spent meditating in dirt or making biscuits in the litter box. Break up your day with some physical activity. Hop on the treadmill, pop out of the mailbox and make the mail carrier wet his or her pants—or just roll over for a start.

---

4. *Hey—can you pass us another crunchy cod stick? Thanks.*

French Women Don't Get Fat . . . But Their Cats Do

Who's more anal-retentive then the French? This is another diet plan perfect for cats who insist on washing their paws in their automatic water dispenser at least three times before eating.

While the commoners among us prefer to think of Persian kitties as little more than puffed-up hussies, the truth is these felines—with their snub noses and glittering tiaras—can teach the rest of us a thing or two about enjoying life without forfeiting culinary excellence. Here, we learn the French way of eating through the eyes of a single feline.

As a slender French *chatte*, Madame Puss was adopted by a typical American couple, discovered crème du Twinkies, and never looked back (mainly because she got so big, it was difficult to turn around). After being referred to one too many times as a "French puff pastry," however, she restored her figure to its pre-soufflé shape. Here then, in her own words, is Madame Puss's story.

The Story of Madame Puss

I was born *un chat simple avec des besoins simples*—a simple cat with simple needs. As a kitten, I lapped crème from a china saucer (I said simple, not heathen), pausing occasionally to tease a stray drop from the whiskers of my brothers or sisters or to have them offer the same service to me. The barn I called home offered a never-ending supply of mice, voles, rabbits, and the occasional barn sparrow who swooped too low at its own peril. (Barn sparrows are stupid creatures.) Weight was never an issue. We ate and played at our leisure, and I can't recall ever leaning over yet another succulent meal of gutted rabbit and thinking, *No, I really shouldn't.* Life was meant for living, and live we did!

That all changed when I came to America. A visiting American couple adopted me, and from my first moments in the states, I knew life would be differ-ent. First of all, there was the tacky home decor, but we won't even go there. (Well, we'll go there a little. Plaid sofas? Sing-

> **EXERCISE TIP:**
>
> In a pinch, bedroom curtains will work in lieu of access to a rock-climbing wall.

ing fish on the wall? *Paper* napkins? The first thing I did upon arrival was to spray the house with disinfectant[5] and take out a subscription in my humans' name to *Architectural Digest* magazine.) But it was the food that stopped me cold.

I was amazed the first night when the man I would come to call "Papa" opened a large resealable plastic bag filled with what I could best surmise was some form of fossilized poop. Worri-somely, the tricolor poop was machine stamped into star and fish

---

5. Okay, cat urine.

shapes, and there was a phrase on the bag I wasn't familiar with: "Tasty meat-like flavor."

Papa opened the bag, presumably to refill the litter box—but no. He scooped a handful into a pink plastic dish with "KITTY" printed on the side and motioned for me to begin eating. I was not even offered tableware. Naturally, I showed him my butt and shunned the "tasty meat-like" poop. For days I endured a hunger strike. Papa threw around phrases such as, "When she gets hungry enough, she'll eat it," but Mama took pity on my plight and began looking for ways to get me to eat.

This is where my weight issues began. Mama snuck me ice cream and cheese, sausage and chicken, potatoes and pancakes—and one glorious day, a deep-fried Twinkie.[6] I grew accustomed to hopping up onto the dining table and eating directly off Mama's plate. She thought it was cute, but we had to pretend around Papa that I never, ever did this. Sometimes I forgot and hopped up anyway, and Mama would have to create a fuss and shoo me away, saying, "What do you think you're doing up here? You know better. Shoo, kitty, shoo." We both got a great deal of amusement at Papa's expense with this charade.

> Treats thrown down the hall contain negative calories because you have to scamper after them.

---

6. If cats ever learn to speak, the first word out of our sweet kitty mouths will be "Twinkies."

It was only during my annual checkup at the vet that I caught a whiff of what such a decadent lifestyle had done to me. "My, what a big kitty," said the vet tech upon my check-in. "What a big kitty with such a sourpuss face."

I immediately marked her for death. But that would have to wait. My first priority was the scale. When I came to America as a kitten, I was a trim six pounds. I stared aghast at a scale that now read fifteen pounds.

"Half of that's probably fur," said Mama to the vet. It crossed my mind to wonder whether she had remembered to pack the frozen Tasty Paws treats I liked so much in her purse as my "You were a good kitty at the vet" reward.

The doctor did not return Mama's smile. "It is *not* fur," she said. "Madame Puss has gained nine pounds in the last year. We need to start watching her diet."

Diet? With my limited English, I was unsure as to the meaning of the word but assumed it had something to do with death. Must someone be sacrificed in order to facilitate my weight loss? Did Mama get to choose whom? Surely we would both miss Papa terribly.

Later that evening, I listened in on a discussion between the two of them.

"Dr. Brewer says we need to watch Madame Puss's diet," said Mama, licking ice cream from her spoon. I sat at her feet, monitoring her every move and willing the spoon to drop from her hand onto the floor.

"You mean *you* need to stop feeding that cat every time she so much as meows at you," said Papa. "You baby her."

"I most certainly do not," said Mama. She reached down and scratched between my ears. "I don't baby you, do I Madame Puss? Do I pussy-wussy-wussy? Who's da best puddy-dat in da world? You are. Yes, you are. Yes, you are."

I impatiently flicked my ears away. Yes, yes, I was well aware of my reigning world status as best kitty ever. What concerned me more was if there was any melted vanilla-bean ice cream left in the bowl or if Mama had polished it off herself. Americans can be so rude.

I jumped up on the arm of the loveseat in which Mama sat.

> Eat seasonal foods: the tender baby mice of spring or the hearty blue jays of fall.

"Look there," said Papa. "That's what I'm talking about. That cat is so fat she practically fell backward trying to drag her ass up onto the chair." (Which is entirely untrue. I *meant* to almost fall backward like that and pinwheel my back paws in the air as I grappled to pull myself up and over the edge.)

"Stop calling her fat. Look at the expression on her face. You've upset her."

"She's a Persian! That cat has looked pissed since the day we brought her home."

Thus began the yo-yo dieting. When Papa was around, we kept up the facade that I ate the diet poop—I mean, food—but it was a culinary free-for-all during the day while he was gone.

"Are you sure you're not feeding that cat on the sly?" he would ask, eyeing what I had come to think of as my very chic American low-slung gunslinger belly. Mama would look offended, then angry, and then would dissolve into tears. Papa would apologize and take her out to dinner, which worked out well for all involved, as I adored the leftovers she slipped me from China World and Taco Palace. All in all, I had a good thing going.

Life would have continued on in this way were it not for two intervening events. One, Papa brought home a dog. And two, the dog had fleas.

Fleas meant flea collars. Except there was not a flea collar large enough to fit around my neck. Even now I recall the burning embarrassment of Mama digging out her old BeDazzler gun and attempting to hot-glue two collars together.

It was then and there that I vowed, *"As God is my witness, they're not going to lick me—except for maybe that hard-to-reach spot behind my ears. If I have to lie, steal, cheat, or kill, as God is my witness, I'll never be hungry again!"*[7]

---

7. *Actually, I vowed to lose a little weight, but I've always wanted to say that line.*

The Diet and Living with *Joie de Purr*

Being unable to fit into a flea collar was the last straw. I knew I had to take matters into my own paws. This is when I developed my strategies for healthy eating and began to live life with true *joie de purr.*

What is *joie de purr*? It's about pleasure. Too many American cats fail to find pleasure in their food. We must ask ourselves why.

Life is about balance. Balancing on ledges and rooftops and the bellies of our humans at two in the morning, yes, but also balance in the sense of everything having a place and purpose in the world. Yet day after day, week after week, year after year, obese American cats face the same bland diet kibble in their dish.

Yet this need not be their fate. There is a world of cottage cheese, melon, deli turkey, and Gerber Turkey & Gravy baby food[8] out there waiting to be savored and salivated over. Are American felines any less deserving of these treats of life simply because they are American and not French? Well, yes, a little. But still, I don't like to see my furry American brethren suffer.

So now, for the first time, I offer my simple strategies for learning to eat, drink, sleep, purr, and—if you haven't been fixed— make love like a French pussycat.

---

8. *Try it. You'll thank me.*

Madame Puss's Secret to Shedding Excess Weight (aka Hair Today, Gone Tomorrow)

STRATEGY #1: RELEASE GUILT

Release any guilt you feel toward food. Guilt is a useless emotion that stifles us emotionally, much as the collar of shame stifles us physically. Ask yourself these questions:

- Do I feel guilt when I shred a new roll of toilet paper conveniently left hanging for my unrolling and tumbling amusement? No.

- Do I feel guilt when the doctor bill comes in for the emergency room visit to treat the sprained ankle suffered by my person when *it was her fault* she didn't see me blending in with the rug at the bottom of the stairs? No.

- And do I feel guilt when I coldcock the neighbor's cocker spaniel when he runs up to greet me with that open, drooly mouth of his? *Mon ami,* no.

> One serving of protein is
> - ¹/₂ a small bunny
> - 1 large or 2 small mice
> - 5 goldfish, skin removed

So why induce feelings of guilt over such a tiny thing as food? Save the guilt for when it's truly necessary—such as when you're caught on the countertop licking frosting off the cake minutes before it's to be served to guests. And remember—the fun of releasing anything is the opportunity to then hunt it down and kill it. Guilt is no different. Release it, hide under the bed until it forgets you're there, then lash out with a lightning-quick paw when it walks by.[9]

STRATEGY #2: BALANCE YOUR MEALS

Use common sense.[10] If you eat a large breakfast, eat a small lunch. If you slip up and eat a big breakfast and lunch, skip dinner. If you really, really slip up and eat a huge breakfast, lunch, and dinner . . . wow, you're on a roll. Keep going!

STRATEGY #3: TREAT YOURSELF

What is life without indulgences? Allowing yourself the occasional treat means you're less likely to go overboard and eat the whole bag of Pounce when you discover it left open in the cupboard. Maybe.

STRATEGY #4: EAT THIRTY-SIX SMALL MEALS A DAY

The trick to not staying hungry is to never let your metabolism drop. Ideally, you'll want to eat about every eight minutes—sooner if you happen to wander past the food dish.

STRATEGY #5: AVOID EXERCISE

It may seem counterintuitive, but exercise makes you hungry, hence you eat more. Some of the thinnest cats we know do nothing but lie

---

9. *If you don't nab guilt, you'll likely still nab an ankle or the dog's tail, which is just as fun.*

10. *It's that sense right behind your Spidey sense, which tells you when a praying mantis is nearby.*

around all day. Be sure to rub this in to the dog, who is being taken out for his third walk of the day. Ha! Loser.

Madame Puss's Magical "Eek!" Soup

I share with you now my hidden weapon. No, not the things I have hidden under the bed. (*Get away from there. Mine.*) The hidden weapon for weight loss is my Magical "Eek!" soup.

What's in Magical "Eek!" soup? Mama unintentionally gave the soup its name when one day in the kitchen a small and nimble *souris* (mouse) scrambled out from underneath the stove. Recalling Strategy #5: Avoid Exercise, I was lying languidly on the floor, bathing, looking up only briefly to watch Mama leap onto a kitchen stool.

> Get up and stretch. Or stay right where you are on top of the heating grate and stretch. But do stretch.

"Eek! Madame Puss! Mouse! Mouse!" Mama pointed at the small gray creature now running in frenzied circles around the base of the stool.[11]

Realizing that something was expected of me in the situation, I paused in my grooming ritual. The mouse skittered over to me and we briefly touched noses. I was instantly charmed. Warm

---

11. Note: *Excessive cardio impedes muscle gain. The mouse would see much faster results from thirty minutes spent weight-lifting.*

kisses on both cheeks or a brief nose touch are so much more refined than the crass American habit of sniffing each other's butts. Sometimes I miss Europe.

The mouse ran back under the stove, and Mama climbed down, using the scolding voice she usually reserved for Papa's dog. I was unaccustomed to being addressed in such a manner and thought briefly of fleeing the room and urinating in her closet. Instead, I chose to resume grooming my private parts.

What it came down to is that apparently *I* was expected to trap, kill, and dismember the *souris*. Although I may have done so indiscriminately in my youth, today I am much more of the "trap—bat around for twenty minutes—then release" mindset. But Mama was adamant, picking me up and placing me in front of the stove as if I were a guardrail or defensive linebacker. (I had lost a good deal of weight by this point, so no fat jokes, please.)

To throw Mama off the track and to keep René safe (yes, I named the mouse), I came up with a solution: Magical "Eek!" soup. Into my water bowl I dragged the following ingredients:

1 dust bunny

$^1/_4$ teaspoon cotton batting from a stuffed mouse toy

$^1/_2$ cup moist food, briefly mouthed, then spat out into water bowl

1 teaspoon blood (nipping the dog while he's sleeping is a quick and efficient, not to mention 100 percent organic means to obtain this ingredient)

Mix all the ingredients well in the water bowl. Once mixed, splash up to half the mixture onto the floor so it appears something was dragged into the food dish against its will. Sit by the water bowl with a warrior-chief look until your human appears.

Important: When your human asks, "What happened here? Did you kill the mouse?" twine between her legs, purring.

There you have it! Magical "Eek!" soup. The "Eek!" comes from the noise your human may still make while under the impression she is cleaning up mouse guts. The Magical part comes from the many, many MANY treats and love you will get for "saving" your person from the horrible mutant mouse creature that lives under the stove. (No offense, René.)

From me to you, much amour . . .
Madame Puss

Eating slowly can help—um, excuse us? We're talking about eating slowly and you are stuffing your face like a chipmunk? As we were saying, eating slowly can—dude, it can't be healthy to stuff that much food into your mouth at one time. Try eating slowly because it—oh my God, okay, the fact that you actually managed to swallow that mouthful was impressive. We totally should have YouTubed that.

Wash Your Paws Twenty Times Before You Exercise: The OCD Cat Workout

We have good news and bad news for you.

The good news is you don't have to join a gym or attend a class to lose weight. (Thank God—can you even imagine the amount of germs floating around a sweaty gym? You'd be licking yourself clean for a month after each visit.)

The bad news is that there are plenty of calorie-burning exercises you can do around the house. Here are some to get you started.

TYPICAL ACTIVITIES AND CALORIES BURNED/HOUR

Screen Door Chin-Ups	425
Chasing the Mysterious Red Dot of Light	300
Vertical Leap onto Drapes	80
Feather Wand Lunges	280
Laps Around the Legs of Anyone Carrying Heavy Bags of Groceries	75
High-Butt Crouch	30

Searching the House for the Perfect Place to Nap	200
Litter Box Squats	89
Tail Raises	130
Stomping on Owner's Face Until He Gets Up to Feed You	50

Do eight to ten reps of each exercise, pausing between each circuit to straighten the sofa cushions and line up the feather wands from biggest to smallest. If the compulsive behavior is really bad that day, just stick with the screen door chin-ups until your eyes bulge and you collapse from exhaustion. There's nothing like cardiovascular failure to work off a little OCD.

> Evaluate your progress. Are you meeting your goals? Exceeding them? Hey—did you even set goals? We told you that was part of the process! Bad kitty!

THE
ADD Cat

If you've ever wondered why Mr. Mittens can eat a thick juicy steak and still lose weight, whereas the cottage cheese you nibbled on earlier went straight to your hips, the answers are here. No, here. On the page. Look here. Quit staring at the ceiling, there's nothing there. Look here. Here-here-here-psssp—kitty, kitty, kitty. Look at me. Look here. Kitty, kitty. Look. Look here. Look at the page! Look at the—oh, forget it.

Here are the recommended diet plans for the ADD cat.

The Paleo Diet

The Zone Diet

Raw Food Diet and the Living Food Movement

The Paleo Diet

The Paleo diet, also known as the caveman or "hunter-gatherer" diet, is an excellent diet option for ADD cats, especially those named Tiger, Leo, or Bone Crusher.

Ancient humans lived a lifestyle of hunting and gathering. Their primary goal on a day-to-day basis was to hunt and gather and sit around the fire arguing over who should be eliminated from *Dancing with the Stars*. Modern-day fans of the Paleo diet spin romantic tales of the days before the agricultural revolution when rough-bearded men wearing loincloths used clubs instead of Cadillac's to kill squirrels and the average diet relied heavily on lean meats, seafood, nuts, seeds, seasonal fruits and vegetables, and, of course, sugar-free JELL-O.

It comes as no surprise that our feline ancestors ate a primarily Paleo diet. But what exactly did they eat? *ScienceNOW* reports that biogeologist Hervé Bocherens analyzed bone collagen from fourteen cave lions, which revealed the big cats' favorite meal to be . . . reindeer.

What does this mean for today's cat? Simple. If you're seeking to lose weight via the Paleo method, you should seat yourself before an eight-course meal starting with an aperitif of Dasher and ending with a dessert tray of Blitzen.[1]

Paleo and the CrossFit Cat

The Paleo diet is most frequently associated with CrossFit. The CrossFit training program has millions of humans—who break a sweat when they reach for the remote—convinced that bench pressing tractor tires and doing backward somersaults into full handstand pushups is within their grasp. Cats know better, which is why you'll never see a feline experience the humiliation of limping into a vet's explaining she threw out her back while attempting to clean and press her own body weight.

CrossFit is also how the whole "black cat crossing your path is bad luck" rumor got started. A prehistoric human crossed the path of a panther, and bad things ensued. Long before the invention of kettleballs and sand bags for fireman carries, the caveman's buddies did a modified CrossFit workout and dragged the mauled body of their buddy back to the cave, where they proceeded to use it in a series of timed burpees and clean-and-press

> Don't skip the most important meal of the day, which would be . . . You know what? To be safe, don't skip any of them.

---

1. *If you want to nosh on a blinking red nose at the end of the meal and call it a cherry, we're willing to look the other way.*

moves. They then spent the evening sipping Chardonnay and playing Pictionary with their friends until someone correctly guessed, "Caveman Bob mauled to death by big black cat!" Thus the rumor of black cats being bad luck was born, along with the CrossFit addiction to burpees.

Rules for the Paleo Diet

- Stick to lean meats. This means no more feeding gourmet cheeses to the mouse under the fridge in an attempt to plump him up before you eat him.

- Seafood is recommended. If you see food, eat it.

- Listen to your body. You may skip meals if you're not hungry.[2]

- Knock over your water dish daily. This doesn't serve any dietary purpose, but it's fun.

- Take measurements. Measure your neck, waist, forepaws, back paws, and—if you're male—the length of your tail.[3]

Common Questions

Do I need to count calories?

Since you can count only to three, it's kind of pointless, don't you think?

Do I need to watch portion size?

Watch? Yes. Do anything about limiting portion sizes? Not so much.

---

2. *We've never known this to happen.*
3. *Tail length has nothing to do with body fat, but we know how you male cats are. Just go ahead and measure it and get it out of your system.*

What is "mindful eating"?

Mindful eating is a very spiritual way of approaching your diet. It's a way in which you focus and pay careful attention to—Oh, you're finished eating? Never mind.

What if I fall off the wagon?

Did anyone see you? If so, act nonchalant, as though you meant to do that. Then sniff the wagon, look bored, and saunter away.

Is there a cheat day allowed on this diet? And what exactly is a "cheat day"?

Cheat days are those days, usually one per week, where you're allowed to eat all the foods you deny yourself the rest of the week. One cheat day per week is allowed on the Paleo diet. You'll find that the trick is staying awake for cheat day, as there's no rule for what constitutes a "day." Fluffy from Wichita, Kansas, once made it 120 hours without sleeping.

Is roadkill allowed on the diet?

Roadkill is an excellent source of protein, and the rubber left from the tire tracks provides fiber. Remember your ethics, however. If you *stumble* across roadkill, fine. But grabbing squirrels by the tail and flinging them in front of tractor-trailer trucks while yelling "Dinner's ready!" is cheating.

PALEO HUMOR

Question: What do you call a vegetarian cat?

Answer: A lousy hunter.

The Zone Diet

If eating the Paleo way isn't enough to satisfy your anal-retentive qualities, you can always try your paw at the Zone diet.

The Zone diet touts itself as a "way of life," but is this really a motivating factor? Consider: cannibalism is a way of life, but you don't see hordes of people rushing to embrace it.[4] Still, if there's a certain event for which you're trying to lose weight, The Zone may be your ticket to staying thin—all while having your cake,[5] eating it,[6] refusing to share the cake with anyone else,[7] throwing away the cake you can't finish because you don't want anyone else to have it,[8] and then going back into the trashcan an hour later and polishing off the discarded cake.[9]

Yes, it's a lot to ask from any weight loss program, but the Zone delivers. (No, they don't deliver pizza. Just weight loss. WEIGHT LOSS. Are you even paying atten—Hey. What are you doing on the phone? Are you ordering? Tell them I want extra pepperoni on my half.)

Before You Get in the Zone

To fully immerse yourself "in the Zone," you need to complete an honest appraisal of your body. To begin, stand in front of a mirror, naked. Yes,

---

4. And if you do, may we suggest you turn and run in the other direction?
5. Mine.
6. All mine.
7. Mine, mine, mine!
8. Still mine.
9. Ha ha! Not yours. MINE.

we're being completely serious. We won't look. Go stand in front of the mirror without your collar, tutu, or lucky batman mask. Next—wait a second. There's some fat tub of lard blocking the view. Go away fat cat! We're trying to see ourselves in the mirror. Shoo! Oh, you want a piece of me? Bring it, tubby. Let's *do* this.

Never mind. We'll look in the mirror later.

Diet Guidelines

The secret behind the Zone diet is *food combinations*. Each meal should consist of 30 percent fat, 30 percent protein, and 40 percent carbs. This is all well and good, except for the fact that cats can't count. And even if we could, we'd count something much more interesting than carbs. Like maybe the number of dust mites in the sunbeam we're lying in.[10] So instead of counting, we've prepared a handy illustration (see next page) of what your plate should look like at each meal:

- *30 percent is protein:* organ meats, gizzards, small (but not large) intestines found in birds, rodents, and small bunnies. Warning: bunny and bird heads are full of carbs—avoid! We suggest offering them to your humans as proof that you're sticking to your diet.

- *30 percent is fat:* bacon, full-fat cream, guacamole, and cheese-filled stink bugs.

- *40 percent is carbs*: kibble, kibble, and more kibble.

---

10. *One...two...thr—ooh look! My tail! Seven...forty-two...*

The Raw Food Diet and the
Living Food Movement

Hmm . . . you're still with us. Amazing for an attention-challenged cat like yourself. But we know why you're here. Yo-yo dieting has got you down. And up. And back down. And up. And back down. Poor ADD kitty—it's your curse in life to be attracted to any object that moves, especially if it's on a string.

But now that you're here and we have your attention—I SAID, now that you're here and we have your—hey! WAKE UP. I mean it. Pay attention to—no, you may not be excused to use the bathroom. You just went. Now get ready as we—will you just leave the fish tank alone, please? And the parakeet. Spit him out, now. (Sigh.) You forgot to take your meds again, didn't you?

Anyway, why raw and living foods? Living foods are good for ADD cats, who lose interest the moment they capture or kill anything (leaving the carcasses of "kill" victims underneath the house to rot and their fragrance to waft up through the ventilation system). It's like the old human saying: "Give a cat a fish, and you feed him for a day. Teach a cat to fish, and you'll regret forever the day you decided to waste money on a koi pond that now serves as little more than a kitty buffet."

And what's the fuss over raw foods? Humans act like they've *never* seen an intestine before. Please. If they can choke down the "food" that comes from the takeout window at Taco Bell, they can deal with your eating the odd eyeball for breakfast now and again. Plus, there's *so much protein* in eyeballs!

Anyway, the first step in any diet is to shift into full-fledged panic the day before the diet officially begins and eat everything—yes, even the really icky kibbles all the way under the fridge—in sight. As you've more than likely already been exhibiting this behavior since, um . . . birth, we're ready to begin.

We've included this chapter because there's a lot of confusion out there regarding the raw food diet and the living food movement. Tribes of cats are embracing—wait. You're right. Cats don't embrace. Tribes of cats are *not entirely shunning* . . . No, that's not quite it. Tribes of cats are *swerving close only to feign interest in something else* . . .

Never mind. Just try the diet. We've pulled together the following Q&A to answer your questions.

What Are Raw and Living Foods?

Shame on you if you must ask this! For too long have you lived the life of the fat, lazy "can you turn up the AC, I almost broke a sweat rolling off the couch" Western cat. You have forgotten the faces of your forefathers, those mighty cats who would *rip the face off* anyone who—well, just off anyone. For penance, go sit beneath the maple tree and allow the squirrels and woodland creatures there to dance upon your face. See if that triggers any thoughts about what may constitute "raw" or "living" food.

Um, I just meant are there any specific principles I should follow if I'm trying to eat raw?

Oh, our bad. Yes: don't cook any food over 116°F. It kills the enzymes. (Sorry about all that face-ripping stuff.)

Is it really safe to eat raw meat?
Two million feral cats can't be wrong.

Is raw fish allowed on these diets?
Not only allowed, but recommended. We've been raiding the Cousteau II fish tank for that very reason. (The fact that we have a personal ven-detta against the puffer fish is irrelevant.)

So . . . uncooked foods are considered "alive"? That's kind of creepy.
Don't get caught up in the language. It's just a way of phrasing things. Like saying the dog has "intelligence."

I still prefer a nice roast in the convection oven.
Infidel!! (Save us a piece.)

As part of the living food movement, can I grow my own food?
You can try, but those baby mice are really hard to bottle-feed.

I was thinking more along the lines of a nice houseplant and an herb garden.
Do you have the moral fortitude to allow the plant to mature before you chew off its leaves? We thought not.

Can I still have my coffee and cigarettes on this diet?
Of course. It's a diet, not hell.

Why is this diet superior to others?
Because it works with, not against, our genetics, feeding us the foods our bodies expect to receive.[11]

---

11. Note: If your body expects to receive a Mouse-Fudge Sundae, prepare to be disappointed.

What is the Tree of Life?

A spiritual, vegan, raw and live food retreat center. Or it may be that weeping willow in your backyard. Seriously, how cool are those trees?

**Not to be gross, but eating a raw diet gives me gas.
How do I deal with this?**

You don't. The smell doesn't bother *you*, right? Others can leave if they find it offensive.

Should I eat more green smoothies?

Careful with the smoothies. Bobtail Bob got his tail caught in a blender and . . . well, now his name is Bobtail Bob.

Does this diet recommend limiting processed foods?

Yes. Wild foods like possum[12] are more nutritious than conventionally domesticated foods. So go ahead, indulge in those wild foods—like that pet ferret you've been eyeing.

Is a plant-based diet healthy?

Cats have known for centuries that a plant-based diet is healthy. Why else do you think we've been eating our humans' precious geraniums?

Sorry, but I prefer my food dead.

No problem. There are plenty of mafia cats for hire, ready to get their paws dirty in exchange for a cut of the meat. Try calicos. Their morals are pretty lax.

---

12. *Have you seen how hideous those things are up close? It's like the universe is telling us it WANTS us to eat the ugly animals and put them out of their misery.*

Exercise for the—Hey Look! There's a Bird! And a Squirrel! And Another Bird!—ADD Cat

With your limited attention span, you crave variety in your workouts. (We know you think you crave only *too*-nah, but you're wrong. Somewhere deep, deep down, you crave working out.) So what are your workout options? Check out the good, the bad, and the "*Oh hell, no!*" options that follow.

Pilates. Anything that starts with the word "pill" makes us nervous. Avoid.

Tae-bo. Great *cat*iovascular workout, offering you the chance to dig in and punch with those claws. Plus, we looooove Billy Blanks.

Catisthenics. Richard Simmons is not the only cat who can rock some leg warmers. Go old school and pull out your '70s sweatbands and your Jane Fonda tapes. Suck in that gut, tuck in that tail, and feel the burn.

Jazzercise. No. Just . . . no.

Yoga. Let your human try to outlast you in "dead-bug pose" or "downward facing dog." Can't be done.

> Want hot abs? Hold "plank" position for as long as possible on the full bladder of any sleeping human.

Resistance Training. Lie on the floor and push yourself to an upright position. Slowly lower back to the floor. Rest for two hours. Repeat.[13]

Spin Class. You've seen what running in circles has done for the dog. Pass.

Purr90X. This workout is all about "muscle confusion," which is what your muscles will surely experience if you start exercising them.

The Thigh Master. What started out as a bet between Mandy the Minx and Bugsy "The Fluffinator" Sphynx over who could get humans to adopt the stupidest form of exercise became an international best seller. Who knew?

High-Intensity Interval Training (HIIT). Cats worldwide embrace this workout that gives us permission to hit people and then—for the cardio benefit only—run away.

Zumba. A congo line of dancing cats? Count us in. (Plus, we like to ogle the Burmese cat in her instructor leotard. *Rowr.*)

13. *For you lady cats concerned about bulging muscles, rise only halfway above the floor and go longer between sets.*

THE Chronic Dieter Cat

Everything in life is a competition. Diets are no different. There are as many diets out there as there are different colored cats. (Although that "all white" cat up the street isn't fooling anyone. Hel-looo? We can see your calico roots, you skank.)

Whether it's who can survive multicat sumo wrestling to be named "King of the Laundry Mountain," or who can twist her head farthest around, Exorcist-style, to clean her back, everyone wants to come out on top. For those of you determined to win the diet wars, here are some options for you.

Master Your Meta*purr*lism

Catty Craig versus Weight Stalkers

Master Your Metapurrlism

We all know them. Those cats who can eat everything in sight and still *lose* weight. Think it's hereditary? Don't be so quick to sniff your butt and chalk it all up to good genes. In her groundbreaking best seller, *Master Your Meta*purr*lism,* renowned feline fitness trainer Jillian "I will hunt you down and kill you if you make me look bad by not losing the weight" *Meow*chaels dishes out the perfect recipe for fast and effective feline weight loss. Her prescription:

- **Remove.** Remove all toxins from the house. This may mean rehoming the dog.

- **Restore.** Restore whole foods to your diet. Still offering the head of birds and small woodland creatures to your humans in hopes that the cholesterol found there will kill them instead of you? Now learn how you can have your bunny and eat him too!

- **Rebalance.** Preferably on a really narrow ledge. This step doesn't have much to do with weight loss, but it's a fun party trick just the same.

We now hand over the chapter to trainer to the stars and really, really fat cats, Jillian *Meow*chaels, already in session with one of her many clients.

> Got yoga? Simple limb expansion techniques can prevent you from fitting into the dreaded carrier that takes you to the vet's office for a weigh-in.

Jillian: You're so fat! You make me want to puke! Why are you so fat? Do twenty pushups while you answer me. Drop! Now!

Cat: I . . . [*gasp, pant*] My mother never loved me . . . and . . .

Jillian: No excuses! Get on the treadmill. Feel the burn. Go, go, go!

Cat: [*Heaving breath*] Please . . . I think I'm dying.

Jillian: It's called tough love, baby. Another set of tricep extensions. Do it! Do it or I'll claw your eyes out.

Um . . . we'll come back to Jillian later. Perhaps after a brief liability talk with our lawyers. For now, let's look at the four phases of Jillian's famous SABR[1] diet tips.

---

1. *Pronounced "saber" as in "Watch out! There's a saber-toothed tiger behind you!"*

Phase 1: Stalk

Before you can lose the fat, you first must corner it, intimidate it, and—in the ultimate kitty throwdown—win a staring contest with it.

Phase 2: Attack

Once the fat is properly intimidated and stunned by your superior tail-twitching ability, you attack it with a combination of diet, exercise, and intense grooming whereby your goal is to actually lick the fat away.

Phase 3: Bat the Fat Around So No One Can Tell Whether You're Serious or Just Killing Time

Just as no one can tell whether you're just playing with that mouse or you really intend to kill him, never let on whether you're serious about losing weight.

Phase 4: Run Away

Treat your diet the same way you do doorbells, vet techs, high heels, and Aunt Dorothy's Doberman (not to mention Aunt Dorothy)—get yourself the hell out of there.

If you find all this too confusing, Jillian suggests you follow these simple rules:

- Eat less.

- Exercise more.

- Eat more fruit.

- But the healthy sugar in fruit will stall weight loss. So avoid fruit.

- Eat whole grains.

- Unless you're kick-starting your diet with a "no carb" period. Then avoid eating whole grains.

- Or, if that's too restrictive, you can eat whole grains, but *only* before 2:00 p.m.

- Unless you're eating low-carb *and* not eating fruit, in which case you can have *some* grains until 2:15 p.m.

- If you exercise, you can eat fruit and grains up to an hour beforehand, even if your weight-loss plan does not allow fruits and grains and it's already 4:30 p.m.

- Unless you're really serious about your weight loss, in which case you'll suck it up and get through the Jillian *Meow*chaels *I'll Beat You Till You Bleed, and You'll Thank Me for It*[2] DVD on nothing more than chicken broth and a piece of steamed kale.

> Fish is a healthy fat, so make yourself a plate of saltwater sushi from the "choose your own fish" tank in the living room.

2. *Also, be sure to purchase Jillian's newest book,* You're So Fat! You Make Me Want to Puke!

Catty Craig Versus Weight Stalkers

In this section we contrast and compare two of the most popular national diets: Catty Craig and Weight Stalkers.

A Chronic Dieter cat is a kitty who has tried everything to shed her muffin top. Liquid diets, calorie restriction (worst three hours of her life, *ever*), low-carb, low fat, pineapple diet (pity the human who had to clean out the litter box *that* month), deal-a-meal, diet buddies, *P90X* (never took it out of the box, but did have fun shredding the box), grain-free, dairy-free, and, in one moment of quiet desperation, the Chronic Dieter cat may have wired her mouth shut with double-sided sticky tape.[3]

None of it worked—or worked for long. Which is why Catty Craig and Weight Stalkers are perfect for hardcore diet kitties. No gimmicks, no fad diets, no fainting into the water dish. Just good old-fashioned starvation-is-the-plan advice.

Target Audience

Both diets market their plans with a specific dieter in mind: essentially, fat, desperate cats.[4]

---

3. *The hair still hasn't fully grown back around her upper lip yet.*
4. *And you think no one ever pays attention to you!*

Celebrity Endorsements

Catty Craig employs the Cheshire Cat from the perennially popular *Alice in Wonderland* with great success. Commercials featuring this celebrity cat emphasize that you too can melt off enough weight so the only body component that remains is your "I'm soooo much thinner and better looking than you are!" grin.

Mr. Bigglesworth, from the *Austin Powers* movie series, has caused some controversy as the Weight Stalkers spokescat. According to Hollywood gossip, this once slightly overweight but healthy-looking feline, now skin and bones, is suffering from anorexia (or a really bad stylist).

before   after

> Slow down between bites. Chew your food. (Obviously this means you'll want to start taking much larger bites of food.)

Still, the amazing transformation has kept kitties hoping to emulate the emaciated look flocking to the Weight Stalkers website.[5]

Philosophy

Catty Craig offers prepackaged food; Weight Stalkers operates on a point system. Both diets claim their goal is for clients to have a healthy relationship with food. This is a challenge, as most cats don't have food relationships, they have food flings—as in, watch me fling my food across the floor before I eat it.

Food Choices

Catty Craig Pro: Prepackaged meals. The human version offers a wide variety of breakfast, lunch, dinner, and snack foods. For cats, it's all kibble, all the time. If you get really hungry, eating the packaging the food came in is allowed.

Catty Craig Con: Sodium content. You may as well set up a salt lick in the dining room.

Weight Stalkers Pro: The diet is based on a points system in which no food is forbidden. We've found the points system to be popular among

---

5. Note: *Garfield was the original Weight Stalkers spokescat, but he was shown the kitty door when it was revealed he'd gained eight pounds after going on a Catty Craig low-cal frozen lasagna–eating binge.*

felines, mainly because cats never properly learn to count: *20 kibbles at 8 points + $^1/_2$ melon at 4 points ÷ 30 calories burned/hour napping for 6 hours = 3.14159 (Pi). What? We're having pie? Awesome.*

Weight Stalkers Con: Having to track the fat, calories, and fiber content of everything we eat gives us a headache. We much prefer to track that little red moving spot of light. Or a foot moving under the bedcovers.

Support

Catty Craig offers a weekly counseling session, by phone or in person. *Note: Catty Craig employs both cat and dog counselors. A sample of your weekly call-in session may go something like this:*

Dog (Counselor): How's your eating been this week?

Cat: Um . . . okay. I'm finding it hard not to snack on my cat treats.

Dog: That is a challenge. Do this—send them to me. I'll eat them for you.

Cat: Thanks. I'm also kind of cheating by eating a lot of turkey and ham.

Dog: Yeah, you're not alone there. Tell you what, send me the deli meats. I'll eat them for you.

Cat: And if I'm being honest, I've been eating a lot of—

Dog: I'll eat it. Send it on.

Cat: But I'm enjoying my Catty Craig prepackaged meals, and—

Dog: Don't eat those. Give them to me. I'll eat them.

Cat: But then what—

Dog: Me. Food. Give *me* all your food. God! I love my job!

Weight Stalkers, on the other hand, offers weekly support groups. Motto: "If you're going to fail, you might as well watch others fail worse, then laugh at them."

Final Comparisons

Catty Craig is right for you if

- You hate to cook and/or are constantly being shooed off the stove.
- You can tolerate being weighed in front of others without having to be wrapped up in a "kitty burrito" for restraint.
- You keep falling off the dieting bandwagon and are too fat to climb back aboard.

Catty Craig is NOT right for you if

- You prefer to catch, kill, and devour your own food.
- You've ever accidentally trapped yourself in the fridge.
- You can't hang with catty counselors.
- You inadvertently arch and hiss every time the bill for your food arrives.

Weight Stalkers is right for you if

- Your goal is a healthy relationship with food instead of the meaningless one-night stands with rotisserie chicken you've been having.

- Counting food points is enough like stalking that you can live with it.
- You don't mind hunting down and killing those present during your weekly "confidential" weigh-in sessions.

Weight Stalkers is NOT right for you if

- You don't like dealing with paid consultants whose job it is to be thinner and prettier than you in the hopes of luring you into buying the two-for-one frozen mouse meal delivery package.

- You dislike mobile tracking tools. The last thing you need is having your whereabouts known.

- You're not open to encouragement from your support group such as "Eat less, fatso" and "Mind if we use your stomach as a serving table for our diet snacks?"

- You freak out when people start screaming "Ferals!" and throwing you and your support group into cages every time more than three of you meet for a weigh-in.

Bottom Line?

They're both cults and probably won't work. Take your pick.

THREE SIMPLE WAYS
TO CUT CALORIES

1. Eat less. (Ha ha—kidding!)
2. Break food into small pieces—crumbs don't have calories.
3. Eat with a friend. If you both eat the same amount, the calories cancel each other out.

The 557th Try Is the Charm: An Exercise Plan for the Chronic Dieter Cat

If you fit the "Chronic Dieter" profile, you need to realize that fit cats aren't so different from you and your lifestyle. They're simply thinner, better looking, and happier, with more attractive friends than you could ever hope to have. That, and their fur always smells good.

Wishing that could be you? The dream is only just beyond your reach—stretch a little farther . . . a little farther . . . a little—oh! You fell. Too bad.

You may never possess the massive amount of self-denial required to be a model-thin kitty, but follow the diet and exercise guidelines detailed here and you'll at least temporarily experience the same wrenching stomach pains that come with being thin and beautiful.

> Writing down what you eat helps you commit to your goal. Or gets you committed. We forget which.

The PURRfect Day

3:30 a.m.–3:35 a.m. Prowl atop bed, leaping over wayward arms and legs.

3:35 a.m.–3:40 a.m. Five-minute cardio blast: knead your paws in steady pumping motion against human's jugular.

3:40 a.m.–3:45 a.m. Plyometrics: leap off bed and dodge pillow thrown your way.

3:45 a.m.–4:00 a.m. Rest: allow heart rate to return to normal, then repeat sequence ten times or until your person gets up to feed you.

4:00 a.m.–4:01 a.m. Breakfast: one full bowl kibble.

4:01 a.m.–4:05 a.m. Leave present in litter box. (Important! Don't skip this step.)

4:05 a.m.–4:20 a.m. Stare forlornly at empty bowl in hopes your people will forget you've already been fed.

4:20 a.m.–5:00 a.m. Tongue bath.

5:00 a.m.–5:30 a.m. Vocal exercises: sit by food dish and meow loudly, glancing pointedly at empty dish.

5:30 a.m.–5:32 a.m. Consume second bowl of kibble.

5:32 a.m.–5:40 a.m. Second litter box deposit (optional).

5:40 a.m.–6:00 a.m. Tongue bath #2.

6:00 a.m.–2:00 p.m. Sleep.

2:00 p.m.–3:00 p.m. Wake up and . . . no, wait. Keep sleeping.

3:00 p.m.–3:10 p.m. Afternoon workout session—chose one of the following options:

- Hide behind door until dog or person walks by, then lash out with paw to scare them.

> Enjoy the occasional cheat day and eat whatever you want. We suggest scheduling cheat days on days that end with a "y."

- Walk halfway down the stairs and meow loudly as if in pain or danger. When someone comes running to see who's attacking you, offer them a blank stare of nonrecognition, then turn and meander back upstairs for your afternoon nap.[6]

3:10 p.m.–5:00 p.m. Burn extra calories by walking into the kitchen every five minutes to see whether your food bowl has been filled. Make anxious *"Ack-ack-ack"* noises when you see that it hasn't been. Remember to *inhale* on the *"Ah"* and *exhale* on the *"ck."*

5:00 p.m.–5:01 p.m. Dinner: one bowl kibble and/or one can moist food.

5:01 p.m.–5:10 p.m. Evening litter box deposit.

5:10 p.m.–5:30 p.m. Evening tongue bath with optional paw pedicure.

5:30 p.m.–Midnight. Nap.

Midnight–3:30 a.m. Exercise time! Play with jingle ball on hardwood floor, swing on drapes, explore any changes or modifications made to kitchen countertops since your last visit twenty-four hours prior, and attack

> How much should the average house cat eat? If you guessed "Meals the size of my paw," good try, but no. Look at the food chart on page 5. The correct answer is: "Meals the size of the Great Pyramid of Giza."

---

6. *Note: At this point, you may find yourself pretty tired. It's okay to supplement your food intake with something as simple as a protein shake. To make: Take one mouse, shake until dead. Add 1 cup water. Blend and consume.*

random bits of clothing left around the house, dragging them into back closets where they'll never be found. Challenge the dog to a wrestling match under your person's bed. Bonus Speed Workout: Run interval laps around the house. Max out your cardio with up/down, up/down, up/down repeats on the stairs.

NOBODY beats baby at getting the treat out of the treat toy. Challenge yourself to knock the kibble out faster each time. Then one day suddenly lose all interest in the toy and refuse to ever touch it again.

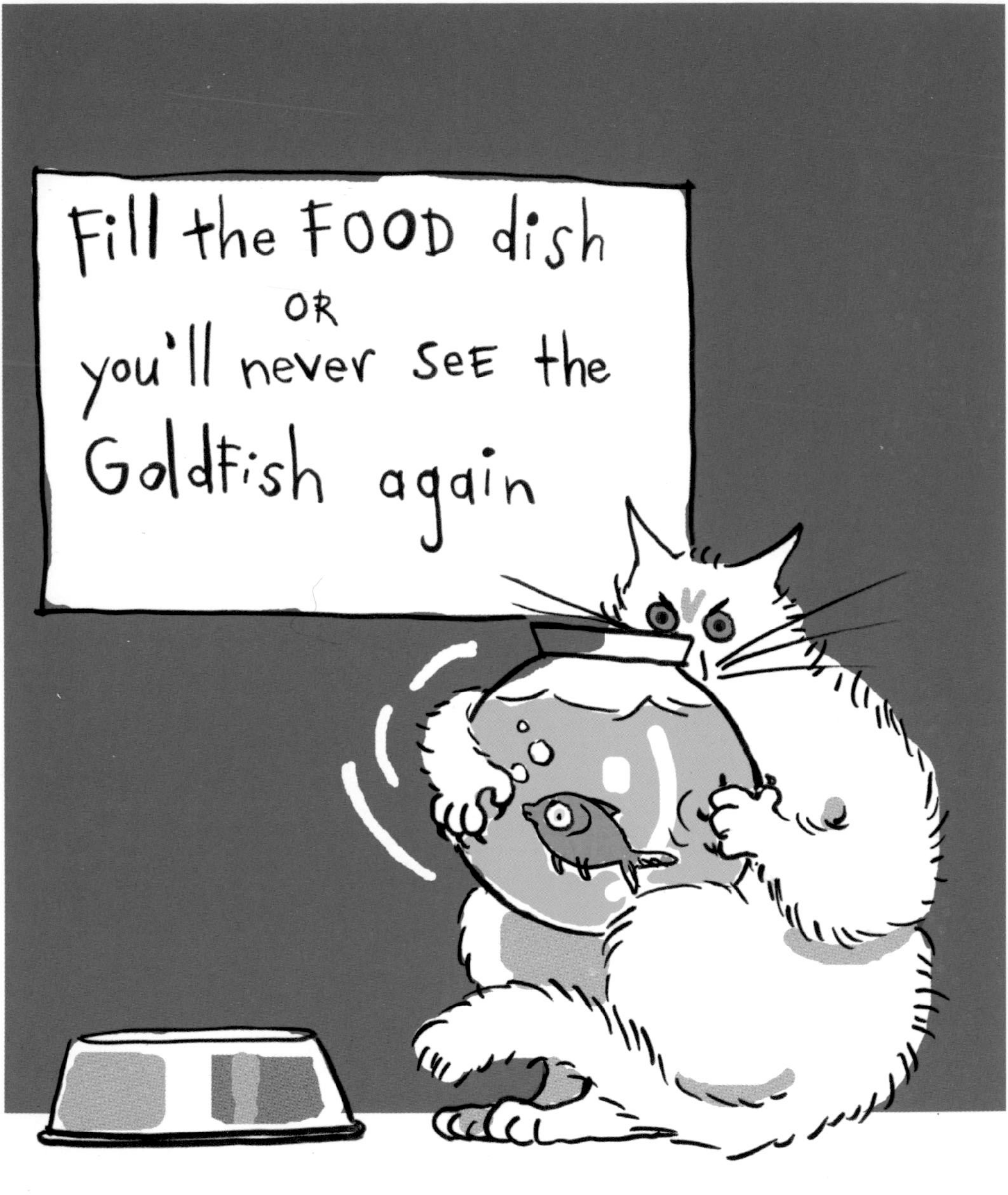
Fill the FOOD dish
OR
you'll never SEE the
Goldfish again

PSYCHO
Kitty

Even basket cases like yourself can stand to shed a few pounds. Because you pride yourself on being unconventional (yes, we're all very impressed with your ability to hang indefinitely from any screen door), here are the diets that will work best for you.

The Mayo Clinic Diet

Cleanses

The Mayo Clinic Diet

This diet became popular among felines once it was observed that "mayo" is the condiment most humans grab right before they pull out the canned tuna. Funded by the Duke's-Kraft-Hellmann's-Miracle Whip Foundation, the Mayo Clinic Diet promotes itself as a weight loss program for life. But over how many lives? Five? Seven? Nine? Relax. Just as the journey of a thousand miles begins with a single step, so does the weight loss of a hundred thousand bits of kibble begin with a single regurgitation on the Oriental rug.

Also, rest assured that there is no need for you to attend a "clinic" as part of this diet. We understand that some of you still harbor grudges from the last time you visited a clinic, and with good reason—apparently they lied when they told you your male parts would "grow back."

How It Works

The Mayo Clinic Diet has two main parts: Lose It and Live It.

Lose It! Jump-start your weight loss (no actual jumping required) and lose as much as 2 kilograms[1] as you focus on adding five healthy habits and breaking five unhealthy habits.

Live It! This is where we try to convince you that eating healthy for life will bring you as much pleasure as scarfing down a vat of taco-flavored kitty Doritos in front of the TV as you sigh over your Netflix DVD of Taylor Lautner in the *Twilight* movies. (Yes, we know he plays a *dog*, but he's still dreamy.)

Phase I: Lose It!

Get ready to add five healthy habits to your life and identify five unhealthy habits worth breaking.

FIVE HABITS TO ADD

1. **Varying your water sources.** The water dish is *so* over. Water from the kitchen faucet or toilet should be available to you on demand. If it's not, yowl like a banshee.

2. **Writing down what you're eating.** Not only will this make you aware of how much you're eating, but it also functions as a grocery list for next week's shopping trip.

---

1. *Is that a lot? A little? Cats can't do metrics, and neither can their American owners, so who knows?*

3. **Fattening up those around you.** Dump some extra kibble into Petal the pug's bowl and watch as you grow slimmer by comparison.

4. **Moving for ten minutes a day.** It need not be ten *consecutive* minutes. Thirty seconds here and thirty seconds there add up.

5. **Eating healthy fats.** The best way to do this is to build a ginger-bread house of candy, then entice mice, birds, and small children inside. Fatten them up, then kill and eat them. (For further diet tips like this, we recommend, *Grimm's Diet Advice: Staying Big, Bad, and Healthy in an Unhealthy World.*)

FIVE HABITS TO BREAK

1. **Consuming white foods.** Luckily, most pet food companies go heavy on the dyes to disguise the color of moth wings and cow gizzards found in commercial pet foods, so breaking this one isn't terribly difficult.

2. **Eating in front of the TV.** You'll find you take in fewer calories if you eat on *top* of the TV. Don't ask us why.

3. **Eating the dog's food.** That's a nasty habit, right up there with smoking or humans attempting to pass off pajama bottoms as pants while shopping at Walmart. Stop it, immediately.

4. **Snacking between meals.** The safer bet is simply to never step away from the food dish. That way, life is just one loooong meal.

5. **Eating out of plastic bowls.** You'll enjoy your meals more if they're presented on delicate china plates and—*HEY! DO NOT PUSH THE*

CHINA PLATE OFF THE COUNTER. I know this is the section on breaking habits, but that doesn't inclu—*I SAW THAT. NOT ONE MORE INCH, MISTER. YOU HEAR ME?* Now move the plate back and away from the edge. Don't you give me that look—you're going to get it. *HEY. HEY!* Oh, you *think you're clever? That's coming out of your allowance, pal.*

> Pack healthy snacks!
> Store mice under the
> fridge or in any cool,
> dark place.

Phase 2: Live It!

Congratulations on making it through Phase 1 without

1. Running in carb-deprivation-induced frenzied circles around the dining room table in hopes of making some pasta fall to the floor.

2. Spraying every "Weight Stalkers Meet Here!" sign you pass on the street.

3. Thinking your parrot on a string toy is talking to you, telling you to *kill . . . kill . . . kill. . . .*[2]

Committing to a healthy life means breaking bad behavior cycles of the past. Just as it took rigorous effort to train yourself *not* to go into full combat mode under the bed every time the doorbell rings (the fact that you no longer automatically dive for your Super Soaker squirt gun is a good sign), so, too, will sticking to a lifetime regime of low-fat mice and soy kibble require your best mental discipline.

---

2. *Hey, no judgment. We've all been there.*

One way to further your efforts is to find new ways to add flavors to your meals. Branch out and try new foods, such as crunchy Parisian duck,[3] smoky Pacific eel,[4] or Australian-inspired kangaroo *amuse-bouche*.[5] Even something as simple as a fish taco (recipe below) can spice up your day.

If all else fails, go ahead and listen to those voices in your head telling you to kill. With a sweet face like yours, no one will ever suspect you were capable of mass murder.

Kitteh's Favorite Fish Taco

Boston mackerel, Spanish mackerel, shad, or the minnows in your human's tank would all be delicious in this taco. Serves 1 kitteh or 4 fully grown men

 2 teaspoons pure cod-liver oil
 1 pound fish
 1/4 cup kalamata olives, pitted and made into a paste
   (chew, then spit back out)
 1 teaspoon pa*purr*ika
 Salt and freshly ground pepper
 8 stone-ground corn or flour tortillas
 2 cups shredded lettuce (use the "low" setting
   on your front claws)
 1 cup chopped tomatoes
 1 cup peeled, thinly sliced cucumber
 4 tablespoons sour cream, for dessert

3. *We've heard it tastes like chicken.*
4. *Anything that slithers will do in a pinch.*
5. *Lucky Aussie cats!*

Preheat the oven to 350°F. You can tell it's ready when you throw a mouse in there and it gives off a popping-sizzling sound.

Heat the cod-liver oil in a skillet. Add the fish to the skillet and cook over medium heat. Turn the fish and continue cooking over moderate heat about 4 minutes longer. Transfer the fish to a plate.

Add the olive paste to the skillet and cook over low heat for 1 minute. Add the pa*purr*ika. Stir with a wooden spoon. Season with salt and pepper.

Warm the tortillas in the oven for 5 minutes. Keep the tortillas warm in foil.

Combine the lettuce, tomatoes, and cucumber.

To serve, throw away the olive paste, tortillas, and vegetable mixture and eat the fish directly off the cooling plate. Finish the meal with the sour cream. *Nom-nom-nom!*

Wine recommendation: Whine for more fish as soon as you lick the plate clean. Repeat process, serve, and enjoy!

> Ask your server—that is, your human—exactly how your food has been prepared. Don't hesitate to send it back if it's not up to your standards.

Cleanses

Okay, psycho kitty—this may be the diet plan for you. Seeing as you're prone to swallowing everything from Siamese fighting fish to shoelaces,[6] a cleanse is exactly what you need. Also, given people's reactions when you pass even the *smallest* bit of gas, we're guessing your body is more "toxic waste dump" than "temple." Cleansing can help. If you're unfamiliar with the concept of cleansing, you're obviously not watching enough *Access Hollywood.* But no worries. This chapter will answer all your questions on topics including

- Reasons to cleanse

- Choosing the cleanse that's right for you

- Cleansing tips

- Whether it's okay to tag-team with another cat and bathe each other[7]

Why Cleanse?

As cats, we've forgotten more about cleansing then most people will ever know.[8] Still, a bit of history is in order.

Cleansing is an ancient tradition by which you rid the body of toxins through a full or modified food fast. That's right, cleansing involves

---

6. *For the last time, stay out of the closet.*
7. *Answer: Yes. But try not to make Yum-mmm sounds while you do it.*
8. *Humans think using a wet paw behind the ear comes natural to us. They don't see the hours of hatha yoga practice we put in to get there.*

giving up food. (Are you okay? You fainted. When's the last time you ate? Two minutes ago? Well, no wonder. You must be famished. Get yourself a snack and then we'll continue.)

Cat cleanses differ from people cleanses. Look at the reasons why people cleanse. Some do it for spiritual reasons, some to do it to detox the body, and others are simply following the latest celebrity trend. Whatever. If cats are going to go for three to ten days without food, it's not because we want to meet God or have a healthy colon. We're doing it because we want to look good naked. *Period.*

Types of Cleanses

Just as all pets are not created equal,[9] so too are all cleanses different. Types of cleanses include the following.

Arise and Shine Cleanse: Requires you to wake up early, so not really practical.

Juice Cleanse: Has you sipping pureed melon and green smoothies. Not bad, until your first stomach rumble kicks in. Which it will, about four minutes into the cleanse.

Raw Food Detox Cleanse: Involves eating only raw food. Challenging if you're accustomed to baking or sautéing your prey in a little EVOO before you eat.

Colonic Cleanse: Best to master the use of the toilet before attempting this one.

---

9. *In case you're wondering, the hierarchy goes: cats → shaky mouse toy → dog → bird → fish → gerbil → human → dead spider.*

Crash Cleanse: Run around the house and crash into things to avoid thinking about how hungry you are. Surprisingly effective.

Liver Cleanse: Eat nothing but liver for forty-eight hours . . . with maybe just a bit of fa-va-va-va beans on the side.

The Master Cleanse: Made popular by the singer Beyoncé, this cleanse involves consuming only lemonade made with grade B maple syrup and cayenne pepper for eight to ten days. Beyoncé told Oprah this diet helped her lose twenty pounds. Then Oprah lost twenty pounds by kicking Beyoncé's skinny little Master Cleanse butt off her stage. Go Big O!

Model Cleanse: Appearance-conscious cats who do stage, TV, and film work swear by the Model Cleanse to flatten their belly before screen time. This cleanse involves eating as much food as you want, then having your assistant Paolo follow you to the litter box and stick his finger down your throat so you regurgitate it all back up. *Note: This cleanse is not recommended for trailer-park cats. It's a glamorous cleanse only if you've got the money to back it up. Otherwise, it's just unhealthy and gross.*

Full Fast: No food for twenty-four hours. Next.

hCG Diet: This liquid diet has you injecting hCG, a pregnancy hormone, while you eat approximately 500 calories per day. hCG has been known to cause "headaches, blood clots, leg cramps, temporary hair thinning, constipation, and breast tenderness."[10] Sounds great. Sign us up.

---

10. Project WatchDog

Skin Cleansing: Instead of eating, groom yourself nonstop for twenty-four hours, swallowing hair to avoid hunger pains. You'll lose weight, and your fur will never look better!

Fat Flush: This cleanse is made challenging by the fact that your humans have kept the lid down on the toilet ever since you became obsessed with dropping your shaky mouse toy in there.

Cleansing Tips

- Before beginning any cleanse, you should consult with your doctor. Ha ha—*not!* Just do what humans do. Commit to your cleanse of choice and deal with the long-term health repercussions later.

- You may want to review basic hazmat training to deal with what you're going to be depositing in your litter box.

- Hallucinations are common during cleansing, so don't panic if you start seeing a chorus of dancing poodles parade down the hall. That's how you know the cleanse is working.

- You may become convinced you're starving. Should this occur, lie down, take a deep breath, then call for Chinese takeout.

Sample Cleanse Diet

Morning: Upon rising, drink 1 cup warm water.

Afternoon: Drink another glass of water at noon. If you feel dizzy, snack on a small pawful of organic sprouts or chew on your human's hair.

Evening: Drink another glass of water.

2:00 a.m.: Eat a large platter of fettuccine Alfredo, using the large side-basket of garlic bread to wipe away your tears of failure.

Morning: Upon rising, drink 1 cup warm water. . . .

Touch My Sweatband and *Die*: Psycho Kitty Workouts

With your disregard for sleeping hours, basic hygiene, and personal space, you're the best of all the personality types when it comes to finding time to squeeze in exercise. You like to feel the burn—Wait. Why is your climbing tree on fire? We'd advise you to consult your physician before undertaking any form of exercise, but knowing the chances of your voluntarily setting paw inside the vet's office, we'll skip it.

Here are some tips for the days when you're feeling less than motivated to climb the stairs *all the way up* to the second floor.

Exercise Tips

- Try a new sport, like paragliding off the kitchen countertops.

- Summit the cat tree. Challenge *accepted.*

- During your workout, ask yourself, "Can I give more?" If the answer is "yes," you're obviously dehydrated and hallucinating. Stop exercising immediately and go eat something.

- Invest in a pedometer. The average American takes 5,117 steps daily. The average Japanese man or woman, 7,168. Cats? 4. If this number seems overwhelming to begin with, bump it down. And remember—this much exercise all at once will take its toll. Allow your body time to recover.

- Exercise first thing upon waking. That way it won't be hanging over your head all day. Plus, you'll have your workout out of the way by 2:00 p.m.

- Get your people to stop leaving NPR on for you in the morning. There simply is no good way to work up a sweat to *All Things Considered*.

- Think mosh pit. Freefall off of doors and cabinets into people's arms. You'll thank us for the adrenaline rush.

- Sometimes a quick three-hour nap is all you need to energize you for the fifteen to twenty minutes you plan to be awake later in the day.

Do you suffer from FOOD ALLERGIES? Many cats have trouble digesting foods such as chicken, milk, or any form of diet kibble. You'll know if you have a food allergy if you regularly throw up a food after eating it. No, wait, that won't really help. You'll know if you feel bloated after . . . no, still no good. Okay, you'll know if your tongue feels kind of rough and . . . shoot. You know what? Let's just assume you don't have any food allergies.

Bonus Section

It's hard for cats to ask for help—it's why we reward firemen with our best "I had the situation under control" sniff when they "rescue" us from trees. Regardless, you may wish to seek the help of your human when attempting to shed a few non-fur-related pounds. Hand this section to your humans, walk away, and let them figure out how to get you to lose weight. Because really, your only concern is what's for dinner.

For Cat Owners:
Putting Your Cat on a Diet in Twenty-One Easy Steps

Step 1: Review your will and check life insurance policies to ensure everything is up to date.

Step 2: Weigh your cat. To do this, weigh yourself first. Step onto scale. Step off scale and check to make sure scale is calibrated to zero. Step back onto scale. Step off scale and go find reading glasses to make sure you're reading the calibration correctly. Step onto scale. Step off scale and remove shoes and socks. Step onto scale. Step off scale and remove all clothing. Step onto scale. Step off scale and remove all jewelry, body piercings, and contact lenses. Step onto scale and hop back off. Pluck eyebrows and do a quick full-body wax. Step back onto scale. Step off scale and carry scale into hallway to ensure you're weighing yourself on a flat surface. Step onto scale. Step off scale and make note to call contractor to replace warped hall floorboards. Step onto scale. Step off scale, get dressed, deposit malfunctioning scale in trash.

Step 3: Drive to nearest Bed, Bath, and Beyond. Snack on baby carrots as you push cart through aisles, looking for new scale.

Step 4: Allow sales clerk to convince you to get a talking scale. Drive home, assemble, and step onto talking scale.

Step 5: Suck down giant cherry Slurpee and gorge on Taco Doritos as you drive back to store to return defective, foul-mouthed scale.

Step 6: On the way home, stop in at local church and light candle to Saint Mochaccino, patron saint of health, skinny lattés, and firm butts.

Step 7: Return home and put out food for obese cat who's feigning death by dehydration because it's been close to an hour since last feeding.

Step 8: Fish original scale out of trash can. Attempt to power sand dents from where you attacked it with a stiletto. Step onto scale.

Step 9: Apologize to local police unit that shows up at your door after neighbors call in a report of someone screaming while being murdered. Make plans to take casseroles to neighbors to make amends. Casseroles always work.

Step 10: Plop down on couch with address book. Call friends and ask them to tell you—honestly—how much they think you weigh.

Step 11: Torch address book. Vow to make new friends, as you hose down living room curtains that caught fire.

Step 12: Sit on couch with large bowl of vanilla ice cream. Allow overweight cat to lick blobs of melted ice cream off your spoon.

Step 13: Assure significant other that you're trying on burkas only as a fashion statement, not because anything is "wrong."

Step 14: Burst into tears when significant other pauses momentarily before responding to your question, "Does this burka make me look fat?" Pry obese cat away from ice-cream bowl and barricade the two of you inside the bathroom.

Step 15: Open bathroom door long enough to hurl demon scale out, narrowly missing confused-looking significant other, who is standing outside bathroom door, surrounded by burkas and tear-soaked chocolate-chip Klondike bar wrappers.

Step 16: Look in bathroom mirror. Take a deep breath. Resolve from here on out to judge yourself solely by inner beauty and the myriad gifts you bring to the world, such as your ability to rock a burka.

Step 17: Open bathroom door. Pick up cat and step on scale. Estimate cat weighs close to eighty pounds.

Step 18: Drive to store to purchase best diet cat food available.

Step 19: Clutch chest when you see cost of premium diet cat food.

Step 20: Feed cat the discount diet kibble you found at dollar store.

Step 21: Write thank-you note to emergency room staff for their excellent attempts at facial reconstruction and for successfully reattaching two out of five of your fingers after feeding diet food to cat.

The End

Appendix

Congratulations! You've made it this far in your weight loss journey. For perspective, most cats don't make it past page 5 without eating themselves into a Pounce-induced sugar coma. To reward you for your stamina, we've included, free of charge,[1] these sections.

Superfuds

Top Ten Tips for Diet Success

Ask Flabby Tabby

1. *Actually, we substantially jacked up the price of the book.*

Superfuds

What are superfuds? Superfuds are nom-noms that are nourishing, nutrient-dense, filling, plush, machine-washable, and—wait, sorry. We're describing our favorite shaky mouse toy.

Okay, superfuds are foods that go beyond normal foods in terms of vitamins, nutrients, and how far they'll travel across the linoleum floor if swatted like a hockey puck with your lethal left paw.

For a food to be labeled a superfud, it must go through superfud training at the League of Justice, bring back the broom of the Wicked Witch of the West, and come to grips with the fact that Darth Vader is its real father. It's a lot to ask from processed kibble, but we think you're worth it.

Ten Superfuds to Incorporate into Your Daily Diet

1. Whatever's in the bowl on your human's lap

2. Goldfish (fresh, not farm raised)

3. Cool Claws ice cream. The packaging says it has nutritional value. What reason would they have to lie?

4. Pepperoni. (It's a vitamin. Just ask the pizza guy; he knows.)

WHAT COUNTS AS ONE SERVING?

A serving is as much food as you can fit into a bowl. To make sure you stay within the serving guidelines, it helps to use the holiday punch bowl as a measuring cup.

---

5. Free-range bunnies

6. Poultry fed an antibiotic-free, hormone-free, non-GMO vegetarian diet and living a stress-free, happy life as certified by the USDA (or Oscar Meyer deli-style thin-sliced honey-smoked turkey breast—whatever's handy)

7. Finches or other winged creatures, including fairies and garden gnomes that congregate around the bird feeder

8. Any gooshy food featuring cute cats in the commercial

9. Wild-caught canned sardines

10. Anything you can paw out from underneath the fridge

Top Ten Tips for Continued Weight-Loss Success

As you move forward in your weight-loss journey—*Oh, for the love of God, we've been through this. It's just a saying. You don't actually have to move. Now come out from under the bed*—you'll want to be sure and revisit the basic tenants of weight loss. Whether you're a comatose kitty, anal-retentive feline, ADD girl, chronic dieting boy, or just a plain old psycho kitty, following these tips will keep you on track for a lifetime (or several lifetimes) of good health:

1. *Purrsonalize your goals.* Take into account how much time and effort you can realistically devote to your weight-loss program, factoring in naps, your couch-shredding commitments, and your bathing rituals. Begin thinking about dieting in five- to ten-minute increments. If you're overcome with feelings of helplessness and nausea, back off to two minutes a week and eat some Pounce kidney-flavored treats to restore your blood sugar level.

2. **Buddy up with a friend and share your weight-loss journey.** The easiest way to do this is to tell a friend he's fat.

3. **Eat only half of what's in your bowl.** Do this unless your humans like to throw out leftover food, in which case shove every last dry kibble you can lay your paws on down your throat.

4. **Buy a low-fat cookbook.** Now shred it. Admit it—that felt good.

5. **Remain realistic.** Weight loss is a process. Aim for a pound a year, and remember—setbacks are inevitable. If you go up five pounds, don't sweat it. You've got eight more lives to work off the weight.

6. **Don't give up!** Unless it's hard. Or you're tired. Or really hungry.
   Or it's a Tuesday.

7. **Avoid reading "cute kittens" calendars.** They'll just make you feel bad about yourself.

8. **If you fall off the wagon. . . .** OMG! Scream for help. Otherwise you'll be left behind, doomed to become an outdoor cat scavenging for scraps. And there is no way your pedicure is going to last if that happens.

9. **Start with a series of small goals that build on each other.** Example: "I will walk by the food dish without stopping to eat a few kibbles." Wait—that may be too hard. Try, "I will *run* by the food dish without—" nope, running wears us out. Okay: "I will *walk* past the room where my food bowl is kept without stopping to—*nom, nom, nom*. What? Can't hear you when I'm chewing all this food."

10. **DO NOT REWARD YOURSELF WITH FOOD.** YOU ARE NOT A DOG.

CAT NIP AND TUCK

Thinking of having a little work done? Botox, collagen, tummy tuck? Just remember true beauty comes from within . . . but a little tail lift never hurt anyone.

Ask Flabby Tabby

Have a question about diet, nutrition, or how to get your favorite jingle ball out from underneath the fridge? Renowned feline health expert and life couch coach Flabby Tabby is here to answer your questions.

Dear Flabby Tabby,
I hear a lot of chatter about feline obesity, but I have found that my girlish curves actually increase my appeal. I may be ten pounds overweight, but I'm proud of my body the way it is. Why should I worry about losing weight?
Signed,
Baby Got Back · Madison, WI

Dear Baby,
Why should you care about obesity? Two words: Diet Kibble.

A little junk in the trunk is hot, but too many spare tires and your vet is going to recommend you reduce your food intake, and then where will you be? Diet kibble is not even fit to feed the *dog,* and he eats poop.

If you don't want to lose your curves, use clothing to hide the weight. An XXL muumuu from Hilo Hattie should do the trick.

Purrs,
Flabby Tabby

Dear Flabby Tabby,
I can't stop eating string! Please help.
Signed,
Strung Out · Dayton, OH

Dear Strung Out,
The first step is admitting you have a problem. The next step is reaching—
no, not swatting, *reaching*—out for help. Please call the national help
hotline at 1-800-BAD-KITY. We'll be pulling for you.
Purrs,
Flabby Tabby

- -

Dear Flabby Tabby,
I'm a black-and-white cat living in the house with a purebred
Persian. "Prissy" makes it clear she thinks she's better than me,
insisting she be the first one fed, combed, petted, and so on. Does
having a pedigree mean she's better than me?
Signed,
Just a Cat · El Paso, TX

Dear Just a Cat,
No! Never let others define you. Listen to me. It doesn't matter where
you come from, what your background is, or where you went to finishing
school. When deciding which cat is "better" than another, there's only
one thing that matters, and that's the answer to the question, "Who's
skinnier, bitch?"

Persians are known to carry their weight in their waist, so emphasize your slim physique with some tight sweaters and then ignore her. All those purebreds are cross-eyed anyway.

Purrs,

Flabby Tabby

Dear Flabby Tabby,

I can't get enough bread into my diet. Sometimes I actually chew through the plastic wrapping to get to the soft, white, doughy goodness. I also get more excited then I think is healthy if someone throws a cooked pasta shell my way. Any thoughts?

Signed,

Carb Kitty · Boston, MA

Dear Carb Kitty,

Let's face it. Cats cannot live on steamed broccoli alone. Enjoy your bread and pasta, but do so in moderation. And by "moderation," I mean "stealth." Carry your ill-gotten bread booty somewhere hidden, like inside the lazy Susan cupboard (just don't get trapped in there like last time) or under the covers at night, so long as you don't mind the smell of feet. Just keep it hush-hush. Remember—calories don't count if no one sees you eat them.

Purrs,

Flabby Tabby

Dear Flabby Tabby,
I'm thinking of undergoing gastric bypass surgery to lose the weight but am wondering—is this sort of extreme weight loss safe?
Signed,
Go Big or Go Home · Las Vegas, NV

Dear Go Big or Go Home,
The last time I underwent surgery, I woke up with no teeth. I'm not even going to tell you what my friend Bill was missing when he woke up. Is surgery really your only option? Have you explored eating less and exercising more?

Bwah-ha-ha—just kidding. Flabby Tabby loves a good joke. No, you should totally go under the knife and keep eating whatever you want. That's what I'd do.

Purrs,
Flabby Tabby

Dear Flabby Tabby,
I participate in cat shows where the pressure to bring home the blue ribbon is intense. Is it ethical if I take supplements to put a little extra shine in my coat?
Signed,
Glowing · Tipp City, OH

Dear Glowing,

That depends. Are you talking about vitamins or banned substances? The United States Anti-Doping Agency (USADA) and the FSST (Feline Substance Sniffing Troupe) have both come down hard on the use of banned substances in cat show competitions. Before you imbibe, think what would happen to your show career if your urine tested positive for a banned substance. And make no mistake—it IS being tested. Why else would people dig your pee and poo out of the litter box twice daily if they weren't testing for illegal substances? What . . . they're doing it to be *nice*?

However, you may want to slip your competition a pill. Remember— it's not whether you win or lose, but how many others you can sandbag along the way. Good luck!

Purrs,

Flabby Tabby

Dear Flabby Tabby,

How much exercise is enough?

Signed,

Would Rather Claw My Eyes Out · Myrtle Beach, SC

Dear Would Rather Claw My Eyes Out,

You should exercise enough that the scale doesn't give an actual gasp of pain when you're set atop it. A few quick laps around the dining room table once a week followed by some box jumps onto the kitchen countertop (that's where the humans keep the good stuff) should suffice. Want more? Tighten your tush by raising your butt to show people every time they enter the room.

Purrs,

Flabby Tabby

Dear Flabby Tabby,

I'm at my wit's end. No matter how hard I try, I can't seem to stay on my diet. I've tried everything, but every time I walk by my food dish, I suck down whatever is in it like a Hoover vacuum. I feel like such a failure. What can I do to change?

Signed,

Never Met a Kibble I Didn't Like · Detroit, MI

Dear Never Met a Kibble,

Don't beat yourself up. (Take it out on the dog. That's what he's there for.) We've all been there. Our ancestors were slim, healthy predators not just by nature, but by need. Think Zumba the Tiger would be able to bag a zebra after noshing on Pounce treats? Not likely.

One thing you can do is to examine your eating triggers—the things that set you off. Examples of eating triggers can be sounds (such as hearing the can opener), activities (such as waking up), or even certain social situations (such as seeing a strange cat in *your* yard). Once you identify your triggers, change them. This may mean you never sleep, look out the window, or use the litter box again, but hey—at least you'll be thin.

Purrs,

Flabby Tabby

About the Author

DENA HARRIS lives in Greensboro, North Carolina, with her husband and two cats—to whom she is allergic (the cats, not the husband). She is the author of *Lessons in Stalking, For the Love of Cats,* and *Who Moved My Mouse? A Self-Help Book for Cats (Who Don't Need Any Help),* which has been translated into six languages. She's held editorial positions at numerous magazines and teaches writing workshops around the nation. Every cat Dena has owned has been full-figured, but they still look fabulous in their collars. They have yet to forgive her for testing the strategies in this book on them.

Visit www.DenaHarris.com.

Index

Published in the United States by Ten Speed Press, an imprint of the
Crown Publishing Group, a division of Random House, Inc., New York.
www.crownpublishing.com
www.tenspeed.com

Ten Speed Press and the Ten Speed Press colophon are registered trademarks of
Random House, Inc.

Library of Congress Cataloging-in-Publication Data
Harris, Dena.
  Does this collar make my butt look big? : a diet book for cats / Dena Harris. — First edition.
     pages cm
  Includes index.
  Summary: "This diet-guide parody shows 'extra furry' cats how to get svelte with kitty-specific versions of popular weight-loss and fitness regimes like the Zone, South Beach, Mayo Clinic, and French Women Don't Get Fat (But Their Cats Do)" —Provided by publisher.
  1. Cats—Humor. 2. Diet—Humor. I. Title.
  PN6231.C23H28 2013
  818'.602—dc23

                                    2012050586

Hardcover ISBN: 978-1-60774-489-4
eBook ISBN: 978-1-60774-490-0

Printed in China

Design by Chloe Rawlins

10 9 8 7 6 5 4 3 2 1

First Edition